(500) DAYS OF SUMMER

(500) DAYS OF SUMMER

Screenplay by Scott Neustadter & Michael H. Weber

Introduction by Marc Webb
Forewords by Michael H. Weber & Scott Neustadter

A Newmarket Shooting Script® Series Book
NEWMARKET PRESS • NEW YORK

Screenplay, Motion Picture Artwork, and Photography ™ & Copyright © 2009 Twentieth Century Fox Film Corporation and Dune Entertainment III LLC. All rights reserved.

Introduction copyright © 2009 by Marc Webb.
Foreword copyright © 2009 by Michael H. Weber.
Foreword copyright © 2009 by Scott Neustadter.

All rights reserved. Used by permission.

The Newmarket Shooting Script® Series is a registered trademark of
Newmarket Publishing & Communications Company.

This book is published simultaneously in the United States of America and in Canada.

All rights reserved. This book may not be reproduced, in whole or in part,
in any form, without written permission. Inquiries should be addressed to:
Permissions Department, Newmarket Press, 18 East 48th Street, New York, NY 10017.

FIRST EDITION

10 9 8 7 6 5 4 3 2 1

ISBN: 978-1-55704-921-6

Library of Congress Catalog-in-Publication Data available upon request.

QUANTITY PURCHASES

Companies, professional groups, clubs, and other organizations may qualify for special terms when ordering quantities of this title. For information e-mail sales@newmarketpress.com or write to Special Sales, Newmarket Press, 18 East 48th Street, New York, NY 10017; call (212) 832-3575 ext. 19 or 1-800-669-3903; FAX (212) 832-3629.

Website: www.newmarketpress.com

Manufactured in the United States of America.

OTHER BOOKS IN THE NEWMARKET SHOOTING SCRIPT® SERIES INCLUDE:

About a Boy: The Shooting Script
Adaptation: The Shooting Script
The Age of Innocence: The Shooting Script
American Beauty: The Shooting Script
A Beautiful Mind: The Shooting Script
The Birdcage: The Shooting Script
Black Hawk Down: The Shooting Script
The Burning Plain: The Shooting Script
Capote: The Shooting Script
The Constant Gardener: The Shooting Script
Dan in Real Life: The Shooting Script
Dead Man Walking: The Shooting Script
Eternal Sunshine of the Spotless Mind:
    The Shooting Script
Funny People: The Shooting Script
Gods and Monsters: The Shooting Script
Gosford Park: The Shooting Script
Human Nature: The Shooting Script
The Hurt Locker: The Shooting Script
Juno: The Shooting Script
Knocked Up: The Shooting Script
The Ice Storm: The Shooting Script
Little Miss Sunshine: The Shooting Script
Margot at the Wedding: The Shooting Script
Michael Clayton: The Shooting Script
Milk: The Shooting Script
The People vs. Larry Flynt: The Shooting Script
The Savages: The Shooting Script
The Shawshank Redemption: The Shooting Script
Sideways: The Shooting Script
Slumdog Millionaire: The Shooting Script
The Squid and the Whale: The Shooting Script
Stranger Than Fiction: The Shooting Script
Synecdoche, New York: The Shooting Script
Taking Woodstock: The Shooting Script
Traffic: The Shooting Script
The Truman Show: The Shooting Script
War of the Worlds: The Shooting Script

OTHER NEWMARKET PICTORIAL MOVIEBOOKS AND NEWMARKET INSIDER FILM BOOKS INCLUDE:

Angels & Demons: The Illustrated Movie Companion
The Art of Monsters vs. Aliens
The Art of X2*
The Art of X-Men: The Last Stand
Bram Stoker's Dracula: The Film and the Legend*
Chicago: The Movie and Lyrics*
Dances with Wolves: The Illustrated Story of the Epic Film*
Dreamgirls
E.T. The Extra-Terrestrial: From Concept to Classic*
Gladiator: The Making of the Ridley Scott Epic Film
Good Night, and Good Luck: The Screenplay and History Behind
    the Landmark Movie*
Hotel Rwanda: Bringing the True Story of an African Hero to Film*
The Jaws Log
The Mummy: Tomb of the Dragon Emperor
Ray: A Tribute to the Movie, the Music, and the Man*
Saving Private Ryan: The Men, The Mission, The Movie
Schindler's List: Images of the Steven Spielberg Film
Superbad: The Illustrated Moviebook*
Tim Burton's Corpse Bride: An Invitation to the Wedding

*Includes Screenplay

CONTENTS

Introduction by Marc Webb	vii
Foreword by Michael H. Weber	ix
Foreword by Scott Neustadter	xi
The Shooting Script	1
Stills	following page 80
Production Notes	111
Cast and Crew Credits	122
About the Filmmakers	128

INTRODUCTION

BY MARC WEBB

Before I read *500 Days of Summer*, I'd completely lost interest in the romantic comedy genre. Somewhere between puberty and when I started paying taxes, I stopped believing in the world these rosy-cheeked girls in cute winter knit caps kept promising me. What did it have to do with me?

When I sat down to read the Xeroxed pages that had already been dog-eared from about three weeks of neglect in my backpack, I wasn't really looking forward to it. It was the title that finally got to me. Needless to say, something clicked.

The writers, Scott Neustadter and Michael Weber, had managed to write an uncynical story for cynical people. Without descending into some oddball high concept, it unearthed some skewed relationships that—God—I hadn't thought of in a while. It was like they were looking into my past and plucking some very private sentiments from some very repressed places. And making jokes out of them. And that's the beauty of it.

We all know Summer because Summer isn't just a girl. She's an event. I met my first Summer when I was seventeen. I won't go into the sordid details, but suffice it to say pretty girls with rebel hearts are in high demand. Some people end up with their Summer. I did not. I couldn't shake that feeling that something had gone horribly, painfully wrong with the universe. Expectations and Reality diverged.

As time wears on, you forget just how acute love can be. When I finally picked up the script, I started to remember. No matter how ridiculous it might seem on the outside—being on the inside is an incredible thing. And that's the secret code of this movie. You see everything from Tom's point of view. Really, you FEEL everything from his point of view. And this curious restriction makes the world come alive. Our movie is not about war. It's not about poverty. It's a playful pop song of a movie. It's about a young man trying to make sense of a young woman.

But these limitations are why the craft of this screenplay is so good. It's a fable conjured from everyday life. Scott and Michael manage to discover all the beauty, pain, humor, drama, and insight from this seemingly small event. The awkwardness of anal girl, the bittersweet irony of the bench scene, the whimsy of Hall and Oates, the incisive, heartrending truth of Expectations vs. Reality. It's all here tied together with a bit of wisdom that hopefully Tom's put some thought into by the end of this story: "She's better than the girl of my dreams, she's real."

I hope you enjoy the read as much as I did.

—October 2009

FOREWORD

BY MICHAEL H. WEBER

I was a Tom before I was a Summer. In one relationship I started as a Tom and ended as a Summer. Most recently I was a Tom once more.

To my surprise and amusement, the release of the movie has led some to consider me an expert on relationships. The idea that I now possess any wisdom regarding the opposite sex or modern romance could not be farther from the truth—just ask any of the Summers and Toms from those aforementioned relationships.

It will be interesting for me, and Scott and Marc as well (and Joe too), to revisit the movie five years from now. In ten years, in twenty. Will any of us know more then? Will we ever have it figured out or will we still be making the same mistakes?

Perhaps being a Tom or a Summer is not a mistake at all. Right now I'm neither. And I miss it. Maybe love is the best mistake you can make.

And if I'm really lucky I'll get a movie out of it.

—October 2009

FOREWORD

BY SCOTT NEUSTADTER

The truth is, none of this was supposed to happen.

I had quit the movie business, where I'd worked as a development exec for the past four years, started the search for a legitimate, practical career, and made peace with the fact that I would never be the writer I had kinda, sorta, always since-I-was-a-fetus wanted to be. And I was fine with this, really, because at that time, at long last, I had finally met THE ONE. I didn't need screenplays and movies, dreams and ambitions. Instead I had this girl and she would save me.

And in a way, I guess, she did.

(500) Days of Summer was written in the aftermath of that relationship (it had to be), and while it's technically not a true story in the strictest sense, believe me when I tell you virtually everything in its pages came true.

Even that last little bit.

—October 2009

(500) DAYS OF SUMMER

by

Scott Neustadter

&

Michael H. Weber

April 16, 2008

NOTE: THE FOLLOWING IS A WORK OF FICTION. ANY RESEMBLANCE TO PERSONS LIVING OR DEAD IS PURELY COINCIDENTAL.

ESPECIALLY YOU JENNY BECKMAN.

BITCH.

FADE IN:

A single number in parenthesis, exactly like so:

(488)

1 EXT. ANGELUS PLAZA - DOWNTOWN LOS ANGELES, CA - DAY   1

And we're looking at a MAN (20s) and a WOMAN (20s) on a bench, high above the city of Los Angeles. Their names are TOM and SUMMER and right now neither one says a word.

CLOSE ON their HANDS, intertwined. Notice the wedding ring on her finger. CLOSE ON Tom, looking at Summer the way every woman wants to be looked at.

And then a DISTINGUISHED VOICE begins to speak to us.

> NARRATOR
> This is a story of boy meets girl.

(1)

2 INT CONFERENCE ROOM - DAY   2

TOM HANSEN sits at a very long rectangular conference table. The walls are lined with framed blow-up sized greeting cards. Tom, dark hair and blue eyes, wears a t-shirt under his sports coat and Adidas tennis shoes to balance out the corporate dress code. He looks pretty bored.

> NARRATOR
> The boy, Tom Hansen of Margate, New Jersey, grew up believing that he'd never truly be happy until the day he met... "the one."

3 INT LIVING ROOM - 1989   3

PRE-TEEN TOM sits alone on his bed engrossed in a movie. His walls are covered in posters of obscure bands. From the TV, we hear: "Elaine! Elaine!"

> NARRATOR
> This belief stemmed from early exposure to sad British pop music and a total misreading of the movie, "The Graduate."

4   INT OFFICE CUBICLE - PRESENT DAY   4

SUMMER FINN files folders and answers phones in a plain white office. She has cropped brown hair almost like a boy's but her face is feminine and pretty enough to get away with it.

>   NARRATOR
>   The girl, Summer Finn of
>   Shinnecock, Michigan, did not share
>   this belief.

5   INT BATHROOM - 1994   5

PRE-TEEN Summer stares at herself in the mirror. Her hair extends down to her lower back.

>   NARRATOR
>   Since the disintegration of her
>   parents' marriage, she'd only loved
>   two things. The first was her long
>   brown hair.

She picks up scissors from the counter and begins to slice.

>   NARRATOR
>   The second was how easily she could
>   cut it off... And feel nothing.

6   INT BOARDROOM - SAME   6

Tom continues to listen to some boring presentation.

6A INT. CUBICLE - SAME   6A

Summer answers a call, takes a message, and walks out of her cubicle down a long narrow hallway.

>   NARRATOR
>   Tom meets Summer on June the 8th.
>   He knows almost immediately...
>   she's who he's been searching for.

CU Summer opening the door to the boardroom, about to come face to face with Tom for the first time.

>   NARRATOR
>   This is a story of boy meets girl.

But before they do,

BLACK.

                    NARRATOR
          You should know up front, this is
          not a love story.

7   INT/EXT OPENING CREDITS SEQUENCE: 7

    SPLITSCREEN OF TOM AND SUMMER AS CHILDREN GROWING UP IN THEIR
    OWN SEPARATE WORLDS, DISCONNECTED AND YET SOMEHOW... NOT.

    For example...

    On the left, Young Tom blows bubbles in a field.

    On the right,

8   INT/EXT FIELD - DAY   8

    Summer runs through a field of dandelions, flying in the wind
    all around her. It should look like the dandelions originated
    with Tom's breath.

    That sort of thing. Anyway...

                                               FADE IN:

(240)

9   EXT DOWNTOWN LA - NIGHT   9

    A 12 year old GIRL rides her bicycle down the block towards
    the Downtown skyline.

9A EXT. TOM'S PLACE - SAME   9A

    The girl arrives at an apartment complex, jumps off the bike
    and races up the front stairs. She rings the doorbell.

10 INT TOM'S PLACE - LATER   10

    PAUL and MCKENZIE open the door. These are Tom's best
    friends. Paul is a doctor and wears hospital scrubs. McKenzie
    works in the cubicle next to Tom.

                    PAUL
          We didn't know who else to call.

    The Girl removes her helmet.

                    MCKENZIE
          It's Amanda Heller all over again.

SFX: a PLATE Crashes O.S.

> GIRL
> You did the right thing. Where is he?

Tom is in the kitchen breaking things and basically going nuts.

As he does, we should notice a few things about his place. One, though it isn't big, it is organized by a master. Two, on the walls, is a series of framed portraits, each one a famous building and its architectural blueprint. As we'll soon learn, Tom has a big interest in architecture.

About to smash a plate on the floor, he's interrupted by:

> GIRL
> Thomas.

Tom freezes.

> TOM
> Rachel? What are you doing here?

Rachel is Tom's 12-year old half-sister.

> RACHEL
> I'm here to help you.

> TOM
> Help me how?

> RACHEL
> First, put down the plate.

CUT TO:

11 INT TOM'S APARTMENT - LATER   11

Tom sits next to Rachel. Paul and Mckenzie sit on either side of them.

> TOM
> I'm gonna be sick.

> RACHEL
> Drink this.

She hands him a glass. Tom drinks it down.

> MCKENZIE
> What is that?

                    RACHEL
          Vodka.

                    TOM
               (grimacing at the taste)
          More.

He gulps another down.

                    TOM
          Does Mom know you're here? It's
          gotta be past 10.

                    RACHEL
          Don't worry about it. Start from
          the beginning. Tell us what
          happened...

Tom takes a deep breath.

12   EXT ANGELUS PLAZA - EARLIER THAT DAY   12

Tom and Summer eat sandwiches on the bench.

                    TOM (V.O.)
          We spent the whole day together.

13   EXT DOWNTOWN FOOD MARKET - EARLIER THAT DAY   13

Tom and Summer walk through the stalls.

14   ENT COFFEE HOUSE - EARLIER THAT DAY   14

Tom and Summer seated outside drinking coffee. He reads the
newspaper, she reads a novel.

15   EXT MOVIE THEATER - EARLIER THAT DAY   15

Tom and Summer walk out of a movie theatre.

16   INT RECORD STORE - EARLIER THAT DAY   16

Tom and Summer shop for music. Tom excitedly shows Summer a
Ringo Starr solo album.

17   INT TOM'S PLACE - SAME   17

                    RACHEL
          And then what?

18   INT DINER - EARLIER THAT NIGHT   18

Tom and Summer in a booth ordering dinner.

                    TOM
              (to WAITRESS)
          You know...let's go crazy, I'll
          have BOTH.
              (to Summer)
          God, I love eating pancakes at
          night. It's like the greatest thing
          ever. How great is this?

                    SUMMER
          I think we should stop seeing each
          other.

19   INT TOM'S PLACE - AS BEFORE   19

                    RACHEL
          Just like that?

                    TOM
          Just like that.

                    PAUL
          Did she say why?

20   INT DINER - AS BEFORE   20

                    SUMMER
          This thing. This whatever it is.
          You and me. Do you think this is
          normal?

                    TOM
          I don't know. Who cares?! I'm
          happy. Aren't you happy?

                    SUMMER
          You're happy?

                    TOM
          You're not?

                    SUMMER
          All we do is argue!

                    TOM
          That is bullshit!

21   INT TOM'S PLACE - AS BEFORE   21

                    RACHEL
          Maybe she was just in a bad mood.

                    PAUL
          A hormonal thing.

                    RACHEL
          PMS?

                    TOM
               (to Rachel)
          What do you know about PMS?

                    RACHEL
          More than you.

                    TOM
          Oh my god.

                    MCKENZIE
          Then what?

22   INT DINER - AS BEFORE   22

                    SUMMER
          This can't be a total surprise. I
          mean, we've been like Sid and Nancy
          for months.

                    TOM
          Summer, Sid stabbed Nancy seven
          times with a kitchen knife. We've
          had some disagreements but I hardly
          think I'm Sid Vicious.

                    SUMMER
          No... I'm Sid.

                    TOM
               (beat)
          Oh so I'm Nancy?!

The Waitress comes out with the food. Tom and Summer stop
their discussion until the meal is served and the Waitress
leaves. Summer starts to eat.

                    SUMMER
          Let's just eat and we'll talk about
          it after.

Without another word she goes back to her pancakes. Tom
watches her eat like this is the worst travesty in the
history of mankind.

                    SUMMER
               (mouth full)
          Mmm, you're so right. These are
          great pancakes!

Tom looks at his food in disgust. He may never eat again.

                    SUMMER
               (innocent)
          What?

Tom stands up to go.

                    SUMMER
          Tom, don't. Come back. You're still
          my best fr---

The sound slows down on the word "friend" (which is an awful, awful word). THE IMAGE FREEZES AND WE ZOOM IN ON TOM'S STUNNED FACE.

23   INT TOM'S PLACE - AS BEFORE   23

Silence for a few beats.

                    PAUL
          Jesus.

                    RACHEL
          Here.

Tom drinks more vodka.

                    RACHEL
          Let's be rational for a second.

                    TOM
          Yes. Let's.

                    RACHEL
          You've broken up with girls before.

                    TOM
          Right.

                    RACHEL
          Girls have broken up with you
          before.

                    TOM
          This is different.

                RACHEL
Why?

                TOM
Cause it's Summer.

                MCKENZIE
Come on, she wasn't <u>that</u> special.

Both Paul and Rachel look at McKenzie with faces that suggest he's wrong there.

                MCKENZIE
So you'll find someone else. Point is, Hansen. You're the best guy I know. You'll get over her.

                PAUL
It's like they say...there's plenty other fish in the sea.

                TOM
No.

                PAUL
Sure they do. They say that.

                TOM
Well they're lying, Paul. It isn't true. This is the girl I've been looking for. I don't want to get over her.
            (beat)
I want to get her back.

(1)

24   INT CONFERENCE ROOM - DAY   24

Tom as we saw him earlier. Bored. In the boardroom. McKenzie is in mid-presentation.

                MCKENZIE
...and if we want the jump on those conservative, right-wing neo-Nazis at Hallmark, maybe playing it safe is the wrong approach. The nuclear family is dead and we need a new holiday to recognize that.

McKenzie holds up a home-made photoshopped family portrait of Martina Navratilova, Ellen DeGeneres, and the kid from "Jerry Maguire".

                    MCKENZIE
        May 21st. *Other* Mother's Day.

The co-workers nod and digest this idea. VANCE is the head of the department.

                    VANCE
        Hmmm. That's an intriguing idea
        McKenzie. Along with Grossman's
        "Magellan Day" I'd say we've got
        some potential here. What do you
        think Hansen? Could you write up
        some prototypes for these?

Tom is about to answer when... the door opens.

                    SUMMER
        Excuse me, Mr. Vance? There's a
        call for you on line 3.

And in walks this girl. Summer. We've met her by now but Tom hasn't. This is the first time. His eyes go wide and from that moment on, he can't take them off her.

                    VANCE
         (to the table)
        Everyone this is Summer, my new
        assistant. Summer just moved here
        from...

                    SUMMER
        Michigan.

                    VANCE
        Right. Michigan. Well, Summer,
        everyone. Everyone, Summer. Excuse
        me, I have to take this.

                    SUMMER
        Nice to meet you all.

Summer gives a little wave before following Vance out. Tom looks like he's just seen God. And on his face, we hear:

                    NARRATOR
          There's only two kinds of people in
          the world. There's women... and
          there's men.

                                                    CUT TO:

25   EXT STREET - DAY - 16MM B&W   25

Summer rides a bicycle down the street.

                    NARRATOR
          Summer Finn was a woman.

FREEZE on SUMMER. (Throughout the following, SUBTITLES will
reveal specifics of the Narrator's points.)

                    NARRATOR
          Height: average.

Titles reveal specifics: <u>5' 5"</u>

                    NARRATOR
          Weight: average.

Titles: <u>121 pounds</u>.

                    NARRATOR
          Shoe size: slightly above average.

Titles: <u>Size 8</u>.

                    NARRATOR
          For all intents and purposes,
          Summer Finn... just another girl.

RESUME regular speed.

                    NARRATOR
          Except she wasn't.

26   **(-5513)**   26

INSERT - Summer's High School Yearbook, littered with letters
from classmates.

                    NARRATOR
          To wit: in 1999, Summer quoted a
          song by the Scottish band Belle &
          Sebastian in her high school
          yearbook.

| 27 | INSERT - Sales Chart of the LP "The Boy With the Arab Strap" by Region, showing an unusual spike in the greater Michigan area. | 27 |

> NARRATOR
> This spike in Michigan sales of their album "Boy With the Arab Strap" continues to puzzle industry analysts.

(-4779)

| 28 | INT COLLEGE CAMPUS - ICE CREAM PARLOR - DAY - 16MM B&W | 28 |

Summer works as a dipper at a busy old timey campus creamery.

> NARRATOR
> Summer's employment at Two Cents Plain during second semester sophomore year coincided with an inexplicable 212% increase in revenue.

In between orders, Summer sneaks a taste of one of the flavors.

(-3)

| 29 | INT APARTMENT - DAY - 16MM B&W | 29 |

Summer is shown a vacant apartment by a SEEDY-LOOKING LANDLORD.

> NARRATOR
> Every apartment Summer rented was offered at an average rate of 9.2% below market value.

(-1)

| 30 | EXT/ INT CITY BUS - DAY - 16MM B&W | 30 |

Summer climbs on to a city bus during a busy morning.

> NARRATOR
> And her round-trip commute to work averaged 18.4 double-takes per day.

Sure enough, several MALE RIDERS and the DRIVER have to look twice.

> NARRATOR
> It was a rare quality, this "esprit special." Rare, and yet something every post-adolescent male has encountered at least once in their lives.

31   EXT STREET - DAY - 16MM B&W   31

Summer continues to ride her bicycle down the street.

> NARRATOR
> That's the third kind of person in the world...

Alone, oblivious, and in her own world.

> NARRATOR
> ... the kind that breaks hearts without trying.

(3 & 4)

32   INT. OFFICE - DAY   32

Tom trying to work. And failing. He turns to McKenzie.

> MCKENZIE
> Dude. I hear she's a bitch from hell!

> TOM
> (disappointed)
> Really?

> MCKENZIE
> Patel tried to talk to her in the copy room. She was totally not having it.

> TOM
> Maybe she was just in a hurry.

> MCKENZIE
> And maybe she's some uppity, better than everyone, superskank.

                    TOM
          Damn.

                    MCKENZIE
          I know. She's pretty hot.

                    TOM
          That sucks, man! Why is it pretty
          girls always think they can treat
          people like crap and get away with
          it?

                    MCKENZIE
          Centuries of reinforcement.

                    TOM
          Like, just cause she has high
          cheekbones and soft skin...

                    MCKENZIE
          ...and really good teeth.

                    TOM
          And those eyes... Just cause of
          that, she can walk around like
          she's center of the universe?

                    MCKENZIE
              (as explanation)
          Women.

                    TOM
          Ugh. You know what? Fine. Whatever.
          I hope I <u>don't</u> meet her.

33   INT. ELEVATOR - LATER   33

     Tom is listening to headphones. Summer enters the elevator
     and Tom actively puts on a show to ignore her. Summer hears
     the music.

                    SUMMER
          The Smiths.

     Tom, pretending not to hear or care, gives her an
     unenthusiastic wave.

                    SUMMER
          I love The Smiths.

     Tom, still pretending, takes off his headphones.

                    TOM
          Sorry?

                    SUMMER
          I said. I love The Smiths. You have
          good taste in music.

A beat as Tom processes this information.

                    TOM
                (amazed)
          You like the Smiths?

                    SUMMER
                (singing)
          "To die by your side is such a
          heavenly way to die." Love it.

The elevator doors open and she gets off.

                    TOM
                (accidentally out loud)
          Holy shit.

(8)

34   INT OFFICE LOBBY - LATER   34

The office is gathered round a 60-something co-worker,
MILLIE, African-American. They toast her with cake and
champagne. A banner above reads "Happy Engagement Millie!"
Tom maneuvers so that he's standing right next to Summer.

                    TOM
          Hey, uh, Summer, right?

                    SUMMER
          Smiths fan.

                    TOM
          That's me. Tom.

                    SUMMER
          Nice to meet you.

                    TOM
          So how's it going?

                    SUMMER
          Pretty good.

                    TOM
          You just moved here, when?

                    SUMMER
          Saturday.

                    TOM
          Wow. And what, uh, brought you?

                    SUMMER
          Boredom, mostly. Got tired of what
          I was doing, who I was with.
          Figured I'd try something new,
          exciting.

                    TOM
               (re: mild office party)
          Well you've clearly come to the
          right place.

Summer laughs. It's adorable.

                    TOM
          What happens when you're bored
          again?

                    SUMMER
               (beat)
          Good question.

They both start to walk. CUT TO:

35   INT OFFICE HALLWAY - SAME   35

                    SUMMER
          And you? Been working here long?

                    TOM
          Eh, you know, bout 4 or 5... years.

                    SUMMER
          Years?! Jesus. So... you've always
          wanted to write greeting cards?

                    TOM
          Oh I don't even want to do it now.

                    SUMMER
               (laughs, it's still
                amazing)
          Maybe you should do something else.

TOM
Yeah. I studied to be an architect, actually.

SUMMER
That's cool! What happened?

TOM
Didn't work out. Needed a job. Here we are.

SUMMER
You any good?

TOM
(points to a framed card)
Well I wrote that one.

SUMMER
(reading)
"Today You're a Man. Mazel Tov on your Bar Mitzvah."

TOM
It's a big seller.

SUMMER
I meant, are you any good as an architect?

TOM
Oh... I doubt it.

SUMMER
Well you are a perfectly ...adequate... greeting card writer.

TOM
That was my nickame in college. "Perfectly adequate" Hansen.

SUMMER
They used to call me "Anal Girl."

Tom does a spit-take and almost chokes.

SUMMER
(explaining)
I was very neat and organized.

There's an awkward silence.

                        SUMMER
            Anyway, I should get back.

                        TOM
            Ok, well, I'll see you around.

She walks back to her cubicle at the other end of the hall.
Tom watches her walk away, completely enamored.

He sits down at his desk and sets out to work. His eyes fall
on a sketch of a house (dated 2001), which is the only
architecture sketch on his wall. Tom has some mojo and starts
a new one. He makes a few moves with the pencil. Looks it
over. And COMPLETELY ERASES WHAT HE DREW. He goes back to his
"real work."

(154)

36   EXT SIDEWALK - DAY   36

        Tom walks alongside his friend PAUL. Nonchalantly, he says:

                        TOM
            It's official. I'm in love with
            Summer.

        Paul looks at Tom, horrified.

                                                        CUT TO:

37   CU - SUMMER'S SMILE   37

                        TOM (V.O.)
            I love her smile.

        CU - SUMMER'S HAIR

                        TOM (V.O.)
            I love her hair.

        CU - SUMMER'S KNEES

                        TOM (V.O.)
            I love her knees.

        CU - SUMMER'S EYES

                        TOM (V.O.)
            I love how one eye is higher up on
            her face than the other eye.

CU - SUMMER'S NECK

                    TOM (V.O.)
          I love the scar on her neck from
          this operation she had as a kid.

CU - SUMMER ASLEEP

                    TOM (V.O.)
          I love how she looks when she's
          sleeping.

CU - SUMMER'S LAUGH

                    TOM (V.O.)
          I love the sound of her laugh.

OVER BLACK, play the opening bars of some over-the-top romantic song.

                    TOM (V.O.)
          I love how I hear this song every
          time I think of her.

CU - TOM, STARING DIRECTLY AT THE CAMERA.

                    TOM (V.O.)
          I love how she makes me feel. Like
          anything's possible. Like, I don't
          know...like life is worth it.

                                                  CUT TO:

39 EXT SIDEWALK - SAME   39

    Paul and Tom. Paul is silent for a beat.

                    PAUL
          Oh this is not good.

(11)

40 INT TOM'S PARENTS' PLACE - DAY   40

    Tom is playing Wii Tennis with Rachel.

                    TOM
          She loves Magritte and Hopper. Oh
          and we talked about "Bananafish"
          for like 20 minutes. We're so
          compatible it's insane! Seriously!
                    (MORE)

TOM (cont'd)
She's not like I thought at all.
She's... amazing.

RACHEL
Oh boy.

TOM
What?

RACHEL
You know...just cause some cute girl likes the same bizarro crap you do doesn't make her your soulmate.

TOM
(beat)
Of course it does.

SARAH (O.S.)
Dinner!

SARAH, 50s, Tom and Rachel's mother, stands in the doorway.

SARAH
Pause and come eat.

They do. Tom enter:

40A   INT. LIVING ROOM -SAME   40A

Tom sits down next to his stepdad Martin, 60s, a quiet, professorial Southern gentleman type.

TOM
Hey Martin.

ANGLE ON RACHEL and Sarah.

RACHEL
He met a girl.

SARAH
(excited)
Yeah?

RACHEL
(grim)
Yeah.

(22)

41 INT - PACMAN CAFE - DAY   41

McKenzie is playing table top Pac Man. Tom and Paul lean against the machine.

> TOM
> It's off.

> PAUL
> What?

> TOM
> Me and Summer.

> MCKENZIE
> Was it ever on?

> TOM
> No. But it could have been. In a world where good things happen to me.

> PAUL
> Yeah well, that's not really where we live.

> TOM
> No.

> MCKENZIE
> So what happened?

> TOM
> You ready for this?

42 INT ELEVATOR - THE DAY BEFORE   42

Tom is alone. The door opens. In walks Summer.

> TOM (V.O.)
> There we are. All alone. Nine more floors to ride. Plenty of time. I figure...this is my chance. If not now when, right?

They ride in silence for a few beats.

> TOM
> Summer...

> SUMMER
> Yeah?

                    TOM
               (beat)
          How was your weekend?

                    SUMMER
          It was good.

43   INT - PACMAN CAFE - AS BEFORE   43

     The friends wait for more.

                    TOM
          You believe that shit?

     Tom's friends look confused.

                    MCKENZIE
          What shit?

                    PAUL
          I think I missed something.

                    TOM
          "It was good." She didn't say "It
          was good." She said "It was good."
          Emphasis on the good. She basically
          said "I spent the weekend having
          sex with this guy I met at the
          gym," the skank. Screw her. It's
          over.

     Tom's friends stare at him. We hear the sound of McKenzie's
     Pac Man being eaten. Everyone's silent, until:

                    MCKENZIE
          What the hell is wrong with you?!

                    TOM
          She's not interested. There's
          nothing I can do.

                    MCKENZIE
          Based on..."it was good?"

                    TOM
          And some other things.

                    PAUL
          Like what, she said "hey" instead
          of "hi" cause that totally means
          she's a lesbian.

                    TOM
            I gave her all sorts of chances.

44   INT OFFICE - DAY   44

Tom types at his desk. Summer approaches the cubicle Tom shares with McKenzie.

                    SUMMER
            I'm going to the supply room.
            Anyone need anything?

                    MCKENZIE
            No thanks.

                    TOM
            I think you know what I need.

There's a beat.

                    TOM
            Toner.

                    SUMMER
            Ok sure, no prob.

45   INT OFFICE - LATE IN THE DAY   45

The office is emptying out. Only a few people remain but Tom and Summer are two of them. Tom takes this opportunity to hit up Itunes on his computer and play a cheesy love song really loud, intending to send Summer a message. He gets no reaction. Tom turns it up. Still nothing. Tom turns it down, defeated.

46   INT - PACMAN CAFE - AS BEFORE   46

                    TOM
            Screw it. I'm done with her. I
            don't need this crap, you know? I'm
            good on my own. Comfortable. Un-
            hassled. People don't realize this
            but loneliness... underrated.

                    PAUL
            You could just ask her out.

                    TOM
            Don't be ridiculous.

(27 & 28)

47 INT OFFICE - TOM'S CUBICLE - DAY   47

Tom sits at his desk with headphones on trying to work. But with Summer down at the end of the hall, he's having a hard time concentrating.

McKenzie shares a cubicle with Tom.

          MCKENZIE
This Friday. All you can Karaoke at The Mill.

          TOM
No way McKenzie.

          MCKENZIE
Come on!

          TOM
They won't let you back in there after last time.

          MCKENZIE
I wasn't that bad.

          TOM
Nooo. You just threw up on the stage, tried to fight the bartender, and threatened to burn the place down. Quiet night for you.

          MCKENZIE
     (reverential)
You saved my life that day.

          TOM
We are not going back there.

          MCKENZIE
It won't be like that. It's a work thing. The whole office is going.

          TOM
I really can't. Even if I wanted to. There's a lot of stuff I gotta take care of.

                    MCKENZIE
          You're not listening to me.

                    TOM
          What?

                    MCKENZIE
          The whole office is going.

Tom looks over to where Summer sits. And the realization
dawns on him...

48   INT KARAOKE BAR - NIGHT   48

Summer is in a back booth with some co-workers when Tom walks
in to the crowded place. McKenzie has the microphone and he's
singing some treacly 80s hair metal ballad. He's real into it
and, well, it's kinda sad. Tom waves to McKenzie and walks
over to the booth.

                    TOM
          Hi.

                    SUMMER
          Hey! They said you weren't coming.

                    TOM
              (shocked)
          You asked if I was --

                    MCKENZIE
              (already drunk)
          Goddamn that song is brilliant!
          What's up Hansen?

Summer sees the next song come up on the screen.

                    SUMMER
          Ooh that's me.

She downs a shot and jumps up on stage.

                    SUMMER
              (into mic)
          Ok. I'm the new girl so no making
          fun of me.

Her co-workers whistle and cheer her on. She takes a deep
breath as her song begins (something exceedingly awesome!)
Summer starts to sing unabashed. Even her uncoolness is cool.
Tom is awed.

49 LATER. Tom sits in the booth with McKenzie (doing a shot) 49
    as Summer chats with co-workers at another table. Tom can't
    help but stare at Summer. She notices and waves. He smiles,
    hopeful that she'll come over. She doesn't. He hides his
    disappointment.

50 LATER. Tom walks back to his table with drinks. Summer is 50
    there in mid-conversation with McKenzie.

>   TOM
>   You were great up there.
>
>   SUMMER
>   Thanks. I was hoping to sing "Born
>   to Run" but they didn't have it.
>
>   TOM
>   I love "Born to Run."
>
>   MCKENZIE
>   Tom here's from New Jersey.
>
>   SUMMER
>   Yeah?
>
>   TOM
>   Lived there til I was 12.
>
>   SUMMER
>   I named my cat after Springsteen.
>
>   TOM
>   No kidding? What's his name?
>
>   SUMMER
>   Bruce.
>
>   TOM
>   (beat)
>   That makes sense.

She laughs. She's really cute when she laughs.

>   MCKENZIE
>   So you got a boyfriend?
>
>   SUMMER
>   Nooo.

Tom shoots daggers at McKenzie for that comment. McKenzie
mouths "what?" Summer sees nothing.

MCKENZIE
Why not?

SUMMER
Don't really want one.

MCKENZIE
Come on. I don't believe that.

SUMMER
You don't believe a woman could enjoy being free and independent?

MCKENZIE
Are you a lesbian?

SUMMER
No, I'm not a lesbian. I'm just not comfortable being somebody's "girlfriend." I don't want to be anybody's anything, you know?

MCKENZIE
I have no idea what you're talking about.

SUMMER
It sounds selfish, I know, but... I just like being on my own. Relationships are messy and feelings get hurt. Who needs all that? We're young. We're in one of the most beautiful cities in the world. I say, let's have as much fun as we can have and leave the serious stuff for later.

MCKENZIE
Holy shit. You're a dude.

TOM
(ignoring him)
So then... what happens if you fall in love?

Summer laughs at this.

TOM
What?

SUMMER
You don't actually believe that, do you?

                    TOM
Believe what? It's love, it's not
Santa Claus.

                    SUMMER
What does that word even mean? I've
been in relationships before and I
can tell you right now I've never
seen it.

                    TOM
Well maybe that's cause --

                    SUMMER
And I know that today most
marriages end in divorce. Like my
parents.

                    TOM
Well mine too but --

                    SUMMER
I read an article in the New
Yorker, says that by stimulating a
part of the brain with electrodes
you can make a person fall in
"love" with a rock. Is that the
love you're talking about?

                    MCKENZIE
Me thinks the lady doth protest too
much.

                    SUMMER
          (matter-of-fact)
The lady dothn't.
          (to Tom)
There's no such thing as "love."
It's a fantasy.

                    TOM
I think you're wrong.

                    SUMMER
Really? And what exactly is it I'm
missing?

                                        CUT TO:

51   AN ANIMATION SEQUENCE, real quick. AN EXPLOSION OF MANY   51
      DIFFERENT COLORS, COMPLETE WITH A CHOIR AND A CHURCH ORGAN
      ALL BUILDING TO A HUGE CRESCENDO.

                                                    BACK TO:

52   INT KARAOKE BAR   52

On Tom:

            TOM
    You'll know it when you feel it.

            SUMMER
        (rolls her eyes)
    How bout we just agree to disagree.

McKenzie senses some discomfort.

            MCKENZIE
    So, uh, who's singing next?

            SUMMER
        (re: singing)
    I nominate Young Werther here.

            TOM
    Nooo. I don't sing in public.

            SUMMER
    Sure you do. You lip-synch to your
    headphones every morning.

            TOM
    I don't...

            MCKENZIE
    You really do.

            SUMMER
    It's ok. I like it. Takes a lot of
    self-confidence to look ridiculous.

            TOM
    Ridiculous?!
        (her smile disarms him)
    Anyway, I'm not near drunk enough
    to sing in front of all these
    people.

            SUMMER
    Bartender!

53 TEN MINUTES LATER. Tom is up there kicking ass. You wouldn't know it till now but he's a ROCK STAR, totally coming out of his shell. He's dancing like Jagger, he's got everyone in the bar singing along. It's a sight to behold. Summer is all smiles watching.

54 LATER. Tom and Summer back at the table. Summer is humming something.

                    TOM
          That's not it.

                    SUMMER
          What is that then?

                    TOM
          I have no idea.

They're both having a good time.

                    SUMMER
          I used to watch it every week.

                    TOM
          Me too. Why can't we think of the
          stupid "Knight Rider" theme song.
          This is gonna bother me for weeks.

                    SUMMER
          Totally.

They share another laugh and then it gets quiet. In that good way.

ANGLE ON McKenzie, wasted, singing the shit out of something patriotic. At any minute he might start to cry.

                    MCKENZIE
          "And I'd proudly stand UP!"
                (aggressive drunk)
          I said stand!

BACK ON TOM and SUMMER, seeing McKenzie start to lose it.

                    TOM
          Here we go.

55 EXT KARAOKE BAR - LATER

Tom helps a nearly comatose McKenzie exit the place. Summer is with them.

                    SUMMER
                (laughing)
            Is he gonna be ok?

                    TOM
            He'll be fine.

A cab arrives. Tom and Summer help McKenzie inside.

                    MCKENZIE
            Hey.

                    TOM
            What's up?

                    MCKENZIE
            Not you. You.
                (beat, to Summer)
            He likes you.

                    TOM
                (quickly)
            Ok, goodnight McKenzie!

                    MCKENZIE
            I mean... likes you, likes you. For
            real. Tell her Tom.

Tom shuts the door on McKenzie as fast as he can. Now it's just Tom and Summer. Tom talks a mile a minute to try and erase McKenzie's last exchange from her mind.

                    TOM
            Sorry you had to see that. Happens
            every time we come here. It's
            unbelievable. Something about that
            guy and singing --

                    SUMMER
            Is that true?

                    TOM
            Yeah, totally, he drinks and he
            just loses his shit.

                    SUMMER
            Not McKenzie. The other thing.

                    TOM
            What thing?

SUMMER
(serious)
Do you...like me?

TOM
Yeah. I like you. Of course I do.

SUMMER
As a friend.

TOM
Right. As a friend.

SUMMER
<u>Just</u> as a friend?

The wheels are spinning in Tom's head. What's the right answer here?

TOM
Yes. I mean... I haven't really thought about... Yes. Why?

SUMMER
Nothing. I just... You're interesting. I'd like us to be friends. Is that ok?

Tom hides his disappointment the best he can.

TOM
Oh yeah totally. Friends. You and me. That's... perfect.

SUMMER
Cool.

Silence.

SUMMER
Well, I'm that way. Good night Tom.

TOM
G'night Summer.

Tom watches her walk away for a beat before he turns to go the other way.

TOM
(under his breath)
Friends. Awesome. That's just great. Well done Hansen, you idiot.

(29)

56 INT OFFICE - COPY ROOM - SAME   56

Tom makes copies. Making copies sure is dull. Summer comes in.

> SUMMER
> Hey there.

> TOM
> (brightens)
> Hi.

Summer makes some copies of her own at the neighboring machine. Tom steals a glance but Summer is all business. Tom thinks about saying something more. Nothing comes. He goes back to copying. They are two people, making photocopies, nothing to see here.

> TOM
> That was fun last --

When suddenly, without his even noticing, SUMMER IS PRESSING AGAINST HIM. And then they're kissing. And it's unbelievable. There's a few seconds where Tom isn't sure if he's dreaming or not. But then he realizes, just like that... somehow he's living his best case scenario.

57 INT TOM'S PLACE - THAT NIGHT   57

Tom answers the door. It's Paul (in hospital scrubs).

> PAUL
> You son of a bitch.

He walks inside without waiting for an invite.

> TOM
> (anxious)
> Shhh.

> PAUL
> The same girl you'd been obsessing over for weeks now?

> TOM
> I have not been...

PAUL
The same girl you said was way out of your league and you wouldn't have a chance with. That girl?

TOM
Paul, seriously...

PAUL
Did you bang her?

TOM
No!

PAUL
Blow job?

TOM
No!

PAUL
Hand job?

TOM
No, Paul, no jobs. I'm still unemployed. We just kissed.

PAUL
Come on, level with me. As your best friend, who tolerated all this talk... Summer this, Summer that, Summer Summer Summer, I mean you were practically stalking her...

TOM
Paul, shhh!

Suddenly, the sound of a toilet flushing is heard. From the bathroom emerges Summer, dressed to go out.

PAUL
Oh.

SUMMER
Hi, I'm Summer.

PAUL
Summer, wow what an unusual name. Tom, how come you've never mentioned you knew such a lovely little lady?
    (off Tom's nasty look)
        (MORE)

                    PAUL (cont'd)
          Or perhaps you have and I've just
          forgot. I mean, with all the women
          in Tom's life it's hard to keep
          track...
                    (not helping)
          Ok, well, I was just... I'm Paul.

                    SUMMER
          Hi Paul.

                    PAUL
                    (not sure what else to
                    say)
          I'm a doctor.

                    SUMMER
          Nice to meet you.

                    PAUL
          Anyway, I'm leaving now. Pretend I
          was never here. Tom, talk to you
          later?... Hey, If any jobs open
          up...

Tom quickly shuts the door on Paul.

                    TOM
          If you heard...

                    SUMMER
          Heard what?

                    TOM
          Excellent. You ready to go.

                    SUMMER
          I'm stalking, STARVING!

Tom realizes she's heard it all. Summer elbows him playfully.

                    TOM
          He exaggerates!

(238)

58   INT IKEA - DAY   58

Tom follows Summer around the store. He eyes a row of sinks.
He turns the handle on one of them but no water comes out.

                    TOM
               (mock surprise)
          Honey, our sink is broken!

                    SUMMER
          Not now, Tom.

                    TOM
               (tries the next few)
          Hmm. Seems like all of our sinks
          are broken.

                    SUMMER
               (serious)
          Just stop it!

Summer walks ahead of him. Tom is surprised by her reaction.
Here's why:

(31)

59   INT IKEA - DAY   59

Tom and Summer browse the maze of furnished rooms.

                    TOM
          What is it you're looking for
          again?

                    SUMMER
          Trivets.

                    TOM
               (indicates an Ikea item)
          How bout a "fluehg?"

                    SUMMER
          A what?

                    TOM
          "Fluehg."

                    SUMMER
          I'm ok for now.

They walk on, stopping at a fully decorated living room. Tom
plops down on the recliner.

                    TOM (CONT'D)
          Ah, home sweet home.

Summer joins in immediately. She sits down on the couch.

                    SUMMER
          Our place is lovely, isn't it?
                (trying to turn on the
                 fake TV)
          Ooh I think "Idol"'s on.
                (fake annoyance)
          Hun, something's wrong with the TV.

                    TOM
                (stands)
          Oh well. Let's eat. I'm famished.

Tom enters the adjacent kitchen, sits down at the table.

                    TOM (CONT'D)
          Smells delicious.

Summer follows, doing her best Donna Reed impression.

                    SUMMER
          I made it myself. It's your
          favorite.

                    TOM
          Bald eagle?

                    SUMMER
          Gross.

                    TOM
          Ever try it?

Summer goes to turn on the sink but no water comes out.

                    SUMMER
          Uh-oh. The sink is broken!

                    TOM
          Not to worry.

He jumps up and pulls her into the next room, another kitchen.

                    TOM (CONT'D)
          That's why we bought a house with
          two kitchens.

                    SUMMER
          You're so smart.

She pulls him into the next room, a bedroom.

                    SUMMER (CONT'D)
            I must have you now.

They embrace. Tom looks over her shoulder to the next room.

                    TOM
            Darling, I don't know how to tell
            you this, but there's a Chinese
            family in our bathroom.

Summer feigns shock. The OTHER CUSTOMERS are looking at them like they're crazy, but they don't care. Tom and Summer collapse onto the bed, laughing.

                    SUMMER
            This is fun. You're fun.

                    TOM
            Thanks.

                    SUMMER
            I mean, I just want to say, up
            front, I'm not looking for anything
            serious.

Tom is a little surprised. The tone of the conversation switches gears a bit.

                    SUMMER
            Are you cool with that?

                    TOM
                (unconvincing)
            Oh yeah.

                    SUMMER
            It freaks some guys out when I say
            that.

                    TOM
                (still confused)
            Not me.

                    SUMMER
            You sure?

                    TOM
            Casual. I get it. See where it
            goes. See what happens. Take it
            slow.

                    SUMMER
          Exactly. No pressure, no labels, no
          obligations. Right?

Tom is visibly disappointed by this but he tries to hide it.
Summer hops off the bed. Tom follows. As they step out of
their fantasy home and back into the store, Summer grabs
Tom's hand. They holding hands. In the real world. Tom is
surprised.

60   INT TOM'S BEDROOM - LATER THAT NIGHT   60

Summer and Tom come bounding in, lip-locked and all over each
other. They fall on his bed and begin undressing each other.
Suddenly, Tom stops.

                    TOM
          I'll be...back in a sec.

He walks into:

60A   INT BATHROOM - SAME   60A

Out of sight, Tom looks in the bathroom mirror.

                    TOM
          Settle. Don't get too excited.
          She's just a girl. Wants to keep it
          casual. Which is why she's in your
          bed right now. Without clothes.
          That's casual, right? That's
          what... casual people do.

He takes a few deep breaths and makes his move.

60B   INT TOM'S BEDROOM - SAME   60B

We watch from behind as he re-enters his bedroom. Where
Summer waits. Under the covers. Naked.

                    SUMMER
          Hi.

                    TOM
          Oh sweet Jesus!

FADE UP: "YOU MAKE MY DREAMS COME TRUE" by Hall and Oates.

                                                        CUT TO:

(32)

61	EXT DOWNTOWN STREET - MORNING	61

It's the greatest morning of all time!

Tom walks down the street. Or, more accurately, Tom struts down the street. People wave as he passes, they clap, they give him thumbs up. Tom points at people as he passes, winking, doing a little shuffle. He is the man. He checks out his reflection in a window. A YOUNG PAUL NEWMAN stares back.

A GROUP of BUSINESSMEN break into a Busby Berkeley-style choreographed dance. A whole parade is forming behind Tom. The POSTMAN, a POLICE OFFICER, the HOT DOG VENDOR, the MICHELIN MAN, the SAN DIEGO CHICKEN, everybody loves Tom today. HALL and OATES themselves walk with Tom singing the song.

Cars stop at crosswalks to let Tom go by. The DRIVERS also pump their fists in celebration of Tom's achievement last night. He walks on, the man.

We notice the sidewalk lights up every time he touches the pavement like in "Billie Jean". CARTOON BIRDS fly onto Tom's shoulder. He smiles and winks at them.

Tom breaks off from the parade as he approaches his office. Steps:

62	EXT TOM'S OFFICE - SAME	62

Tom walks into the building.

63	INT ELEVATOR - SAME	63

Tom steps into the elevator, and as the doors close, the music stops abruptly.

(268)

64	INT TOM'S OFFICE - DAY	64

The elevator opens to reveal Tom, looking very unkept, unshaven, and unwell. He walks to his cubicle.

CUT TO:

65	LATER. Tom is staring off in the direction of Summer's office.	65

REVEAL a NEW SECRETARY sitting there.

The New Secretary is more than a little skeeved out by Tom's stare.

SFX: a "New Message" chime. Tom gets excited. He's been waiting for this.

ANGLE ON THE COMPUTER -- it's just spam. Tom balls his fist in anger. Totally stressed. McKenzie pops up from his station.

> MCKENZIE
> So... get her back yet?

> TOM
> Working on it.

> MCKENZIE
> Maybe you should write a book.

> TOM
> Huh?

> MCKENZIE
> Henry Miller said the best way to get over a girl -- turn her into literature.

> TOM
> That guy had a lot more sex than me.

And then... another "New Message" chime.

> TOM
> Here we go!

Takes a deep breath, swallows, and opens the email. And it's from her. McKenzie maneuvers to look over Tom's shoulder. As he reads:

> SUMMER (V.O.)
> So great to hear from you. I can't this week but maybe next? I hope this means you're ready to be fr--

On that word again, the sound slows down to reinforce its power. THE SCENE FREEZES AND WE QUICK ZOOM in on Tom's face. Hearing "friends" is like a punch in the gut. RESUME NORMAL SPEED. McKenzie pats Tom on the shoulder. Tom scratches his head, takes a second to think about it. Clicks delete.

BLACK.

FADE UP: Someone is humming the "Knight Rider" Theme song.

(45)

66 INT COPY ROOM - DAY 66

Summer is on her cell phone in the office copy room, humming the theme song.

> TOM (V.O.)
> That's it!

McKenzie enters and sees her singing into the phone. Turns without a word and leaves.

67 INT TOM'S CUBICLE - SAME 67

Tom listening to her sing, loving every minute of it. McKenzie comes over.

> MCKENZIE
> Your girl is losing it.

(59)

68 INT. DOWNTOWN ART GALLERY - DAY 68

CU: a painting -- some avant guard surrealist depiction of two dogs humping.

ANGLE ON Summer and Tom looking curiously at it.

> TOM
> Very... complex.

> SUMMER
> Complex. Yes.

CU: a second painting which is nothing but red.

ANGLE ON Summer and Tom looking at it with the same expressions.

> SUMMER
> In a way, it speaks so much by saying... so little.

> TOM
> I feel the same way.

CU: a third painting which could only be, well, poop.

ANGLE ON Summer and Tom, still perplexed but trying.

They say nothing, until:

>   TOM
> You wanna go to the movies?

>   SUMMER
>   (relieved)
> God yes!

69   EXT. MOVIE THEATER - LATER   69

The marquee reads "Part Vampire. Part Giant. 'VAGIANT!'"

70   INT. MOVIE THEATER - CONT.   70

The theater is packed. Everyone is laughing and screaming and throwing popcorn. Tom and Summer are having a great time.

(87)

71   INT RECORD STORE - NIGHT   71

Tom and Summer wander through the aisles.

>   TOM
> There's no way.

>   SUMMER
> Why not?

>   TOM
> "Octopus's Garden?" You may as well
> just say "Piggies?"

>   SUMMER
> I told you. I love Ringo.

>   TOM
> You're insane.

>   SUMMER
> Why?

>   TOM
> Cause <u>nobody</u> loves Ringo.

                    SUMMER
          That's what I love about him.

Summer drags Tom into the curtained-off "Porn" section. She picks up a box, "Sweet and Shower."

                    SUMMER
               (flirtatious)
          This got great reviews.

72   INT. TOM'S APARTMENT - LATER   72

Tom and Summer get comfortable. Both are excited and looking forward to this. The movie starts, the credits roll. Tom and Summer start to make out a bit, both keeping an eye on the TV.

                    SUMMER
          Looks easy enough.

73   INT. SHOWER - LATER   73

We just see the curtain, but we can see their silhouettes behind it. Summer and Tom are trying to have sex in the shower. They're trying to stabilize themselves, to grip something so as not to fall, elbows are flying, it's a mess.

                    TOM
          Ow!

The curtain rips and the bar comes crashing down. They fall on top of each other laughing. Shower sex is hard.

(95)

74   EXT DOWNTOWN STREET - DAY   74

Tom is pointing out to Summer some of what he loves about the city.

                    TOM
          If you're just looking at the
          street, I admit -- doesn't look
          like much. But if you look up...

They do. And it's beautiful.

75   EXT ANOTHER STREET CORNER - DAY   75

Summer and Tom in front of the famous Fine Arts building.

                    TOM
          The guys who designed this...
          Geniuses.

76   EXT ANGELUS PLAZA - LATER   76

Tom and Summer sit down on a bench. This is the same bench they sat at on the very first page (and will sit at again), overlooking the city.

                    TOM
          This is my favorite spot.

They take in the expanse. Old, almost dilapidated Downtown LA. Definitely not scenic. Mostly parking garages.

                    SUMMER
          This?

                    TOM
          Yeah.

                    SUMMER
          Tell me why.

                    TOM
          I don't know...

                    SUMMER
          Sure you do.

                    TOM
          No, it's... it's hard to explain.

Summer shoots him a look, encouraging him to go on.

                    TOM
          You really wanna know?

                    SUMMER
          Absolutely.

                    TOM
              (points)
          You see that building with the
          orange hue? That's been there since
          1911. Over there, that's the
          Continental. LA's first skyscraper.
          Built in 1904. People think of LA
          as this place with no history, you
          know, where nothing is real. That's
          only cause they're not paying
          attention.

                    SUMMER
              (points)
        What's that?

                    TOM
        That's... a parking lot. Most of
        that is parking lots. But there's
        so much beauty too. See, if it was
        me...

                    SUMMER
        What?

                    TOM
        I just... I'd make sure people
        noticed. That's what I would do.
        Integrate the buildings better.
        Play off the facades, maximize the
        light capacity, there's really so
        much...

                    SUMMER
        Show me.

                    TOM
        Hmm?

                    SUMMER
        Don't just talk about it, Tom.
              (beat)
        <u>Do it</u>.

Summer gives him a pen from her purse and the underside of
her arm. Tom thinks about this. Then he starts to draw a
sketch on her skin. We catch her watching his face as he
draws. She's attracted to his enthusiasm.

                    TOM
        So we start with this, right
        here...

(PRODUCTION NOTE: Put AUTUMN somewhere subtle in the
background.)

(109)

77   INT SUMMER'S APARTMENT - NIGHT   77

Music plays as Tom follows Summer inside her apartment for
the first time. The significance of this isn't lost on him.

                    SUMMER
          It's a bit of a mess.

                    TOM
          That's ok.

                    NARRATOR
          For Tom Hansen, this was the night
          where everything changed.

Tom takes in the unpacked boxes, the photographs, wall
decorations, books, CDs, everything that one can't know about
a person outside their bedroom.

                    NARRATOR
          That wall Summer so often hid
          behind, a wall of distance, of
          space, of "casual"... that wall was
          slowly coming down. For here was
          Tom, in her world, a place few had
          been invited to see with their own
          eyes...

(From the disparity of stuff, we should get a sense that
unlike Tom, whose room reflects his interest in architecture,
Summer is all over the place).

78   QUICK CUTS FROM DURING THE NIGHT: 78

- Summer laughing at something Tom said.

                    NARRATOR (CONT'D)
          ... and here was Summer, wanting
          him there. Him, no one else.

- Tom and Summer in bed together.

                    SUMMER
          Tornados?

                    TOM
          Weird, right?

                    SUMMER
          You live in LA. Why would you dream
          of tornados?

                    TOM
          I don't know but I do. Tornados.
          And my teeth falling out.

                    SUMMER
          I have that too! That's so funny.

                    TOM
          What about you?

                    SUMMER
          Earthquakes.

                    TOM
          For real?

                    SUMMER
          No. I don't remember most of my
          dreams.
                (beat)
          There's this one... nevermind. ...

                    TOM
          What?

                    SUMMER
          It's nothing.

                    TOM
          I wanna hear.

                    SUMMER
                (beat)
          I dream about flying.

                    TOM
          You do?

                    SUMMER
          Not really flying. More like...
          floating. Like, it starts out I'm
          running really fast.

- Summer playfully sticking her tongue out at Tom and
the two of them fake wrestling.

                    SUMMER
          And then the... terrain... gets all
          rocky and steep. But I don't slow
          down. I just climb higher and
          higher with every stride. Before I
          know it, I'm... floating.

- Summer wiping an eyelash from Tom's cheek.

                    SUMMER
          I'm going so fast my feet don't
          even touch the ground. I'm up in
          the air and I'm... I don't know...
          free. It's this incredible feeling.

– Summer and Tom continuing their intimate conversation.

     TOM
  Sounds amazing.

     SUMMER
  But then I look down. And the
  minute I do... everything changes.
  There I am... I'm floating, high
  above the earth, nothing can touch
  me, right? I'm free and I'm safe
  and it hits me, just like that...
  I'm completely, utterly, alone.

It's silent for a beat.

     SUMMER
  And then I wake up.

     NARRATOR (V.O.)
  As he listened, Tom began to
  realize that these weren't stories
  routinely told. These were stories
  one had to <u>earn</u>. He could feel the
  wall coming down. He wondered if
  anyone else had made it this far.
  Which is why the next five words
  changed everything.

     SUMMER
  I've never told <u>anyone</u> that.

Tom's face changes as he's hit with a realization. Yes,
Summer has chosen to let him in. It's beginning. On Tom's
face, determined to close the deal...

     TOM
  I guess I'm... not just anyone.

(116)

79 INT – PACMAN CAFE – DAY   79

Tom plays the table top Pac Man game with his friends
surrounding.

     PAUL
  So what <u>are</u> you exactly?

     TOM
  I don't know.

                    PAUL
          Are you her boyfriend now?

                    TOM
          It's not that simple.

                    MCKENZIE
          Sure it is.

                    TOM
          Like, are we "going steady?" Come
          on, guys. We're adults. We know how
          we feel. We don't need to label it.
          "Boyfriend, girlfriend." That stuff
          is very... juvenile.

Beat. Tom looks up from the game.

                    MCKENZIE
          You're so gay.

                    PAUL
          You really are.

                    TOM
          Ok. Number one. Your last
          girlfriend was Amy Sussman in the
          7th grade and you "dated" for an
          hour. And you... you've been with
          Robyn and no one else since you
          were ten. I hardly think you two
          are the authorities on modern
          relationships.

(118)

80   EXT FIELD - DAY   80

Tom is watching Rachel play soccer from behind the players'
bench. A whistle blows and Rachel comes back and sits down.
She's the authority.

                    TOM
          So what should I do?

                    RACHEL
          You should ask her.
               (off his silence)
          What?

                    TOM
          (beat)
     "Why rock the boat?" is what I'm
     thinking. Things are going well. If
     we start putting labels on it,
     that's like the kiss of death. Like
     saying to a girl "I love you."

                    RACHEL
     I know what you mean. That's what
     happened with me and Sean.

                    TOM
     Who the hell's Sean?

                    RACHEL
     My boyfriend before Mark.

                    TOM
     Who the f--! Never mind. So you're
     saying...

                    RACHEL
     I'm saying... you <u>do</u> want to ask
     her. That's obvious. You're just
     afraid you'll get an answer you
     don't want which will shatter your
     illusions of how good everything's
     been these past few months. Now if
     it were me, I'd find out <u>now</u> before
     you show up to her place and she's
     in bed with Lars from Norway.

                    TOM
     Who's Lars from Norway?

                    RACHEL
     Just some guy she met at the gym
     with Brad Pitt's face and Jesus's
     abs.

                    TOM
     Bastard.

The whistle blows again and Rachel gets up to go back on the
field.

                    TOM
     Coach, wait! We're not done.

                    RACHEL
               (calling back)
          It's easy Tom... just don't be a
          pussy!

On Tom, we:

                                             CUT TO:

81   INT TOM'S CAR - LATER   81

     Tom and Summer driving. Tom is very conflicted and we can see
     it in his face. They're silent a few beats, before:

                    SUMMER
          Are you ok?

                    TOM
          Yeah.

                    SUMMER
          You sure?

     He's not. He clenches his teeth. And begins...

                    TOM
          Summer, I've gotta ask you
          something.

                    SUMMER
          Ok.

                    TOM
          What are we doing?

                    SUMMER
          I thought we were going to the
          movies.

                    TOM
          No, I mean... what's going on here?
          With us.

                    SUMMER
          I don't know. Who cares? I'm happy.
          Aren't you happy?

                    TOM
          Yeah.

                    SUMMER
          Good.

                    TOM
                (beat)
            It's just...

                    SUMMER
            Ooh!

Summer has noticed the song on the radio.

                    SUMMER
            Oh my god. We totally can't talk
            during this song.

Tom listens and Tom watches Summer listening. There's something about this moment, the way she sings along, the way her eyes close during certain notes, the way her smile rises and falls like she could cry at any minute from being overwhelmingly happy or just simply overwhelmed. Tom is powerless to stop his feelings for this girl. We know, as well as he does: he will not press the issue tonight.

The car drives into the 3rd street tunnel and disappears into the dark.

(366)

82   EXT PARTY - NIGHT   82

The song from the car is now playing in the background of a rooftop party. Tom and Summer are there, in conversation with several PARTYGOERS.

                    PARTYGOER
                (to Tom)
            And what is it you do?

                    TOM
            I write greeting cards.

                    ANOTHER PARTYGOER
            No shit.

                    SUMMER
            He could be a great architect if he
            wanted.

                    PARTYGOER
            That's... unusual. What made you go
            from one to the other?

                    TOM
          Well I thought, why make something
          totally disposable -- like a
          building -- when I could make
          something that lasts forever. Like
          a birthday card.

     Everyone laughs at this. Everyone but Summer.

83   TIME CUTS reveal that Tom is against the railing by   83
     himself. Meanwhile, Summer is talking with, laughing with,
     drinking with, and possibly flirting with many of them. Tom
     notices, smiles, pretends it doesn't mean anything, but he's
     clearly jealous. Not in a sexual way but of the <u>attention</u>
     they're getting from her. He misses that attention.

     # (269)

84   CU - TOM. HE'S A MESS.   84

                    TOM
               (into CAMERA)
          I hate Summer.

85   CU - SUMMER'S SMILE (as before)   85

                    TOM (V.O.)
          I hate her crooked teeth.

     CU - SUMMER'S HAIR (as before)

                    TOM (V.O.)
          I hate her 1950s haircut.

     CU - SUMMER'S KNEES (as before)

                    TOM (V.O.)
          I hate her knobby knees.

     CU - SUMMER'S EYES (as before)

                    TOM (V.O.)
          I hate her lopsided, asymmetrical,
          cock-eyed head.

     CU - SUMMER'S NECK (as before)

                    TOM (V.O.)
          I hate that centipede-shaped scar.

     CU - SUMMER ASLEEP (as before)

                    TOM (V.O.)
               I hate the way she sleeps.

CU - SUMMER'S LAUGH

                    TOM (V.O.)
               I hate the way she laughs.

OVER BLACK, play the opening bars of that same over-the-top romantic song.

                    TOM (V.O.)
               I HATE THIS EFFING SONG!

86   CU - TOM.   86

REVERSE ANGLE on A BUS FULL OF PEOPLE, terrified of this raving lunatic.

                    BUS DRIVER
               Son, you're gonna have to exit the
               vehicle.

(185)

87   INT GOLDEN GOPHER - DOWNTOWN BAR - NIGHT   87

Summer and Tom stand by the bar.

                    TOM
               London 1964. Those girls knew how
               to dress. Nowadays it's all giant
               sunglasses, tattoos, little
               handbags with dogs in them. Who
               okayed this?

                    SUMMER
               Some people like it.

                    TOM
               I like how you dress.

                    SUMMER
               Darn. I was just thinking about
               getting a butterfly on my calf,
               bout yay big...

                    TOM
                    (beat)
               Please don't.

                    DOUCHE (O.S.)
               Yo.

And now this tall, well-built, GOOD-LOOKING DOUCHEBAG GUY has suddenly appeared next to them.

                    DOUCHE
                 (to Summer)
               How's it going?

                    SUMMER
               K.

Tom puts his hands in his pockets and watches this exchange go down. Not sure what else to do. At this point he's more amused than concerned.

                    DOUCHE
               You live around here?

                    SUMMER
               Yeah not too far.

                    DOUCHE
               I've never seen you here before.

                    SUMMER
               You're not too observant.

                    DOUCHE
               Ha. That's funny. You're funny.

Tom smiles to himself. This guy's a tool. Nothing to worry about.

                    DOUCHE
               So, uh, let me buy you a drink.

                    SUMMER
               No thank you.

As she answers Summer gives a quick glance over to Tom. The Guy notices. Up to this point he had not connected the two of them together.

                    DOUCHE
               Are you with this guy?

Tom realizes he has to sort of say something now.

                    TOM
                 (beat)
               Hi. I'm Tom.

                    DOUCHE
          Whatever.
               (to Summer)
          Come on, one drink. What are you
          drinking?

                    SUMMER
          Sorry, no thank you.

                    DOUCHE
          You're serious? This guy?

                    TOM
          Hey buddy --

                    SUMMER
               (to the Douche)
          Don't be rude. I'm flattered, I'm
          just not interested. Now why don't
          you go back over there and leave us
          alone, ok?

                    DOUCHE
          It's a free country.

Summer and Tom make eye contact again, as if to say "now what?" After a beat:

                    DOUCHE
          I can't believe this is your
          boyfriend.

And with that in the air, Tom, panicked, decides to cut the silence. All the pent up uncertainty and confusion, coupled with the challenge to his manhood in front of the woman he loves, all manifests in one single, solid, almost automatic RIGHT CROSS TO THE GOOD LOOKING DOUCHEBAG'S FACE.

Which connects spot on and sends the Douche reeling.

Both Douche and Tom wince at the pain (Douche's chin, Tom's fist).

There's a beat of calm where Tom is actually sorta surprised. And then the Douche spins around and starts PUMMELLING TOM.

                                                            CUT TO:

88   INT SUMMER'S APARTMENT - LATER   88

Tom follows Summer inside. He still holds a bandage to his nose and his shirt is bloody. Still, he feels pretty great about it.

                    TOM
          I mean, that was crazy! Did you see
          that? I was like Ali. I just wound
          up and
               (tries to make a fist)
          -- ow! Jesus.

Tom's fist is still totally sore. It's around this point that Tom notices Summer hasn't been talking to him.

                    TOM
          Hey.
               (nothing)
          What's the matter?

                    SUMMER
          I just... I can't believe you.

                    TOM
          Can't believe me?

                    SUMMER
          You were so completely uncool in
          there.

                    TOM
          Wait. You're mad? I just got my ass
          kicked for you.

                    SUMMER
          Oh was that for my benefit? You
          were protecting me?

                    TOM
          Yes I was.

                    SUMMER
          Well next time Tommy, don't. I
          don't need your protection.

                    TOM
          I just --

                    SUMMER
          Look. I'm tired. Can we talk about
          this tomorrow?

Tom, completely exasperated, throws his hands in the air and walks towards the door. But then he turns around.

                    TOM
          No, screw this. I'm not going
          anywhere til you tell me what's
          going on.

                    SUMMER
          Nothing, Tom. Nothing is going on.
          We're just...

                    TOM
          What...? What are we?

                    SUMMER
          We're just fr--

                    TOM
          Oh no... Oh no you don't! Don't
          even think about saying that!
          You're gonna pull that shit with
          me? This is not how you treat your
          friends. Kissing in the copy room.
          Holding hands in Ikea? Shower sex?
          Friends, my balls.

                    SUMMER
          I like you, Tom. I just don't want-

                    TOM
          Well guess what? It's not up to
          you! I get a say in this. And I say
          we're a couple goddamit.

                    SUMMER
          Tom --

Tom makes a dramatic exit. We track with him:

89   INT STAIRWELL - SAME   89

     Racing down the stairs, muttering angrily to himself the
     whole time. He passes TWO GIRLS walking up.

                    TOM
          Anyone else wanna kick my ass
          tonight?

90   EXT SUMMER'S APARTMENT - SAME   90

     Tom exits in a huff. He walks down the street, continuing to
     talk himself into a fury. Then he stops.

                    TOM
          No, you know what...

Tom turns around. He has more to say. He marches up to Summer's door and is going back up there.

Except the door is locked. Tom's shoulders sag. He has no choice but to buzz.

          SUMMER (THROUGH BUZZER)
Hello?

          TOM
It's me.

Beat.

          SUMMER (THROUGH BUZZER)
Can I help you?

          TOM
        (reluctantly)
There's more I want to say.

Beat. Beat. Beat. Beat. Beat. Beat.

Finally, he hears the buzzer. He opens the door, we follow him:

91   INT STAIRWELL - SAME   91

As he walks back up the stairs. There's a lot of fucking stairs.

92   INT HALLWAY - OUTSIDE SUMMER'S APARTMENT - SAME   92

By the time Tom gets up there, he's a little winded. Summer meets him in the doorway.

          SUMMER
Yes?

          TOM
        (beat)
I can't remember now.

          SUMMER
I'm going to sleep.

          TOM
Fine.

          SUMMER
Fine.

Beat.

                    TOM
          This was very different in my head.

                    SUMMER
          I bet you get that a lot.

And with that she shuts the door, leaving Tom outside to pick up the pieces.

SPLITSCREEN - INT. BOTH APARTMENTS - THAT NIGHT

93   <u>Left</u>: Tom tosses and turns in his sleep.   93

94   <u>Right</u>: Summer lies awake, staring at the ceiling.   94

95   <u>Left</u>: Tom picks up the phone. Is about to dial when he   95
     stops himself and hangs up.

96   <u>Right</u>: Summer looks at her phone, willing it to ring. It   96
     doesn't.

97   INT TOM'S BEDROOM - HOURS LATER   97

Tom is awakened by the doorbell. He gets up, concerned, and goes to answer it. It's Summer.

                    SUMMER
          I shouldn't have done that.

                    TOM
          What?

                    SUMMER
          Gotten mad at you. I'm sorry.

                    TOM
          Summer... we don't have to label
          what we're doing. I just... I need -

                    SUMMER
          I know -

                    TOM
          Consistency. I need to know you
          won't wake up tomorrow and feel a
          different way.

                    SUMMER
          I can't promise you that. Nobody
          can.
               (beat)
          I can only tell you how I feel
          right now... or I can show you.

She comes in and kisses him. He thinks about it for a second. Is this enough? Damn it, she wins again. He shuts the door in our faces.

98 INT TOM'S BEDROOM - MORNING   98

Still bruised Tom and Summer, early in the morning.

> TOM
> Her name was Amanda. And I just...
> what can I say, I really liked her.

> SUMMER
> You loooved her.

> TOM
> (re: back of his hand)
> Don't make me use this.

> SUMMER
> Bring it!

Tom tickles her. She squirms out of it. They return to position.

> TOM
> I thought I loved her. Now I don't know.

Silence. Tom decides to change the subject. Sort of.

> TOM
> What about you? You ever even have a "boyfriend?"

> SUMMER
> Well... yeah, of course.

> TOM
> Tell me about em.

> SUMMER
> Oh no way.

> TOM
> Why?

> SUMMER
> There's nothing to tell.

> TOM
> Come on, I'm interested.

                    SUMMER
            You wanna go there?

                    TOM
            Why not? I can take it.

                    SUMMER
            Alright... well... there was Markus
            in high school.

99   INSERT: Still photograph of MARKUS. Or at least how he
     appears in Tom's mind. Arm cocked, about to throw the winning
     touchdown pass.

100   TOM
            Quarterback slash homecoming king?

                    SUMMER
            He was a rower. Very hot.

                    TOM
            And what happened to Markus?

                    SUMMER
            He works for the Republican party.
            Very successful. Just not for me.

                    TOM
            And then?

                    SUMMER
            Well, for a short time in college,
            there was Charlie.

101 INSERT: Still photograph of CHARLIE. As Tom envisions
     him. Playing the guitar on stage in some hair band,
     surrounded by groupies.

102   SUMMER
            She was nice but...

Tom's eyes bug out.

                    SUMMER
            Then there was... my semester in
            Spain. Fernando Belardelli. AKA
            "The Puma."

103 INSERT: Still photograph of THE PUMA. A swarthy Spaniard
     posing in front of a Vespa moped in tight Gucci pants, his
     boner clearly trying to escape.

104   TOM   104
           The Puma?

           SUMMER
           Yeah, cause, you know...

Tom has no idea. And he doesn't want to know.

           TOM
           And that's it?

           SUMMER
           The ones that lasted.

           TOM
           What happened? Why didn't they work
           out?

           SUMMER
           What always happens... life.

On TOM. Silent for a few beats. Did he want to hear that?

(141)

105   EXT ANGELUS PLAZA - DAY   105

Tom and Summer walk through the park. It's a beautiful day
out, mobbed with pedestrians. They're in mid-conversation.

           TOM
           That's the dumbest thing I've ever
           heard.

           SUMMER
           It's not dumb. It's awesome. Trust
           me.

Tom is reluctant to participate in whatever this is.

           SUMMER
           I'll go first.

After a beat:

           SUMMER
              (whispers)
           Penis.

Tom looks at Summer like she's insane.

SUMMER
Come on.

Tom rolls his eyes.

TOM
(only slightly louder)
Penis.

SUMMER
(slightly louder)
Penis.

TOM
(slightly louder)
Penis.

SUMMER
(louder)
Penis.

TOM
There's kids around.

SUMMER
No there isn't.

Tom looks over his shoulders. People are gonna hear him now.

TOM
Penis.

SUMMER
(no holds barred)
Penis!

TOM
Shhh, Jesus!

They get dirty looks from some passersby. Summer thinks this is hilarious. She has no shame.

TOM
You having fun?

SUMMER
Oh yeah.

TOM
This is what you used to do with the Puma, isn't it?

SUMMER
God no... We rarely left his room.

TOM
(loud)
Penis!!

Everyone turns and looks at them. Summer cracks up. Tom does too. The game is kinda fun.

TOM
(to ONLOOKER)
Sorry. Tourette's. You know how it is.

SUMMER
(yelling)
Penis!

TOM
She has it too.
(louder even)
Penis!!

SUMMER
(really loud)
Peni--

Tom grabs Summer and throws her over his shoulder in an effort to silence her. He spins her around in the air.

SUMMER
Ok ok!

Together, they fall to the ground. Tom covers her mouth with his fingers.

TOM
Are you finished?
(off her nod)
Promise?
(more nodding)

Tom releases her. They lay on the ground, face to face. It's a charged moment between them. Summer smiles.

SUMMER
(the loudest yet)
Pee --!

But Tom is quick. He covers her mouth with his. And on Tom and Summer, kissing, laughing, rolling around on the ground, we hear:

                    MAN'S VOICE (V.O.)
                  (in French w/ Subtitles)
                 "Misery. Loneliness. Pain."

MUSIC CUE: A MELODRAMATIC INSTRUMENTAL which plays over the
following:

106   OMITTED   106

107   OMITTED   107

108   OMITTED   108

109   OMITTED   109

110   OMITTED   110

111   OMITTED   111

(273-286)

111A INT. MOVIE THEATRE - DAY   111A

      Tom has taken refuge in a movie theatre, the light of the
      film reflecting on his face, and we hear:

                    MAN'S VOICE (V.O.)
                  (in French w/ Subtitles)
              This was his life now. Each day,
              the same dull throbbing ache of a
              wounded heart.

                                                            CUT TO:

111B THE BLACK AND WHITE FILM   111B

      REVEAL Tom has put himself in the film that he's watching. In
      this shot, he is dressed like Belmondo in "Breathless"
      complete with cigarette and hat. He makes serious faces at
      the camera.

                    MAN'S VOICE (V.O.)
                  (in French w/ Subtitles)
              He is a song without melody. A bird
              without wings. Or anything
              purchased at Radio Shack.
                        (beat)
              He is broken.

                                                            CUT TO:

ANOTHER SHOT FROM THE BLACK AND WHITE FILM

111C   EXT STREET - DAY   111C

Sad Tom wanders down a desolate street holding a balloon. There is no one else around save a SAD-LOOKING MIME. JUMP CUTS of Tom as he walks, the Sad Mime following closely all the while.

> MAN'S VOICE (V.O.)
> (in French w/ Subtitles)
> More than broken, he is alone. For who but he could ever understand the tangled, twisted mess of his now empty soul?

The Mime's actions get increasingly more bizarre. He requests the balloon from Tom.

> MAN'S VOICE (V.O.)
> (in French w/ Subtitles)
> Now his only friend is grief. The grief that he carries like a badge, a badge he can never take off...

Tom gives him the balloon. The Mime almost immediately lets go of it.

> MAN'S VOICE (V.O.)
> (in French w/ Subtitles)
> ... which, come to think of it, is pretty unusual for a badge. Not so much like a badge, then, more like a tattoo. A tatoo he can never take off.
> (beat)
> Yes, that's better.

Tom looks at the Mime incredulously as if to say, "what the fuck was that for, Mime?"

                                                        CUT TO:

111D   ANOTHER SHOT FROM THE BLACK AND WHITE FILM   111D

This is the famous Bergman PERSONA symmetrical face blocking shot. Half of Tom's face looking at us and half of Summer's looking off to the side, set against a dramatic black backdrop.

> MAN'S VOICE (V.O.)
> (in French w/ Subtitles)
> In any case... suffering.

                    TOM (ON SCREEN)
          Suffering.

                    MAN'S VOICE (V.O.)
                (in French w/ Subtitles)
          Endless suffering.

                    SUMMER (ON SCREEN)
          So much suffering.

                    MAN'S VOICE (V.O.)
                (in French w/ Subtitles)
          The kind of suffering that never
          ends.

                    TOM (ON SCREEN)
          Suffering.

                    SUMMER (ON SCREEN)
          Suffering.

                    MAN'S VOICE (V.O.)
                (in French w/ Subtitles)
          A shitload of suffering is what I'm
          saying.

                                                  CUT TO:

111E   FINAL SHOT OF THE BLACK AND WHITE FILM   111E

     Tom playing chess against DEATH. Only it isn't Death. It's a
     half-naked cherub with wings and an arrow -- it's CUPID.

                    TOM
                (in French w/ Subtitles)
          Your move.

     Cupid thinks for a beat then makes his move. He wins the game
     and knocks over Tom's King.

                    CUPID
                (in French w/ Subtitles)
          Better luck next time... bitch.

     Tom hides his head in his hands. A loser at love yet again.
     At which point the film burns out.

                                                  BACK TO:

111F   INT MOVIE THEATRE - SAME   111F

Tom who has dozed off wakes up from the sound. Looks at his watch. Grabs his coat. Nods a thanks to the projectionist and leaves. Back to reality. Sort of.

(293)

FADE UP: "YOU MAKE MY DREAM COME TRUE" by Hall and Oates.

112   EXT STREET - MORNING   112

Now everything fucking sucks!

Tom walks down the street. Or, more accurately, Tom sulks down the street. Though it's sunny and warm, Tom is a sad, broken man and the world is an awful place. Tom checks out his reflection in a window and an ugly cartoonish face glares back.

Tom walks by a COUPLE making out on a bench. He grimaces.

He walks by a sign that says "TODAY ONLY: FREE BEER." He doesn't even stop.

Cartoon Bird returns but Tom swats it away.

The WORLD'S MOST BEAUTIFUL WOMAN stops to ask him for directions. He doesn't even look up.

Tom's parade of supporters shake their heads and give him disapproving looks. The Cartoon Bird takes a cartoon shit on Tom's shoulder. Tom tries to kill the bird. Can't even manage that.

(303)

113   INT OFFICE - DAY   113

Tom sits at his desk, miserable. A NEW SECRETARY, not Summer, comes by.

      NEW SECRETARY
  Tom. Mr. Vance would like to see
  you in his office?

114   INT VANCE'S OFFICE - DAY   114

Tom has been called into the Principal's office.

VANCE
Sit down, Tom.
    (he does)
Has something happened to you recently?

TOM
What do you mean?

VANCE
A death in the family, someone taken ill...anything like that?

TOM
No.

VANCE
Look, I don't mean to pry. Does this have something to do with Summer leaving.

TOM
Who?

VANCE.
My assistant.

TOM
    (faking badly)
Your...?

VANCE.
Tom...everyone knows. Nevermind. The reason I'm asking...lately your work performance has been... a little off.

TOM
I'm not following.

VANCE
For example, here's something you wrote last week...
    (reads from a card on his
     desk)
"Roses are Red, Violets are Blue... Fuck You Whore." Now, most shoppers on Valentine's Day ---

TOM
    (almost hopeful)
Mr. Vance... are you firing me?

                    VANCE
          No, no, no. Relax Hansen. You're
          one of the good ones.

                    TOM
          Ok. Well, I'm sorry. Things for me
          have been a little difficult.

                    VANCE
          That's ok. I understand that. I was
          just thinking... perhaps you could
          channel your energy into... this.

He hands him some sympathy cards.

                    TOM
          Funerals and sympathy?

                    VANCE
          Misery, sadness, loss of faith, no
          reasons to live... it's perfect for
          you. Whaddaya say? Good? Good. Now
          back to work you go.

He quickly ushers him out of the office. Tom stands face to face with a framed card of two hearts holding hands. The card reads "I. Love. Us." Tom stares at it for a second.

(167)

115   INT OFFICE - DAY   115

Tom is wandering through the office whistling.

                    MCKENZIE
          Don't you have like twenty cards to
          write by Friday?

                    TOM
          Nope. All finished.

                    MCKENZIE
          Can you help me? I've run out of
          ways to say "congrats." I've got
          "Good job," "well done," "way to
          go"... About it.

                    TOM
          Why don't you try... "Everyday you
          make me proud. But today, you get a
          card."

                    MCKENZIE
                (beat)
            Shit. That's not bad.

                    TOM
            No worries.

Tom walks by the room marked "Religious." He's about to keep going when he pauses.

116   INT RELIGIOUS HOLIDAYS WING - LATER   116

Workers are again all gathered around Tom.

                    TOM
            Did you try... "Merry?"

                    ALL
            Whoa/Perfect/Yes!

                    TOM
            What else you got?

                    EMPLOYEE #1
            Passover.

                    TOM
            "Alay-bin oyf dine kupp. Hag
            Sameyach, meyntayera kinder."

No one knows what the hell he just said except for one Employee who bursts out in tears of joy.

117   INT WEDDINGS AND ANNIVERSARIES SUITE - LATER   117

All of the people who work in here are MIDDLE AGED WOMEN. Currently, they are standing around one desk where Tom sits helping everyone with their cards.

                    MILLIE
            We've been stuck on this for an
            hour.

Tom looks it over. Thinks.

                    TOM
            Here's what I would say...

Tom sees the side of Summer's face across the room.

                              TOM
                    "I. Love. Us."
                         (beat)
                    What do you think?

                              MILLIE
                         (clutching her heart)
                    It's beautiful.

The Women are so moved they might faint.

118   INT OFFICE HALLWAY - LATER   118

Tom passes Summer at her desk. She waves. He waves back. He's so in love with her.

(306)

119   EXT. DOWNTOWN STREET - DAY   119

Tom, unshaven, un-showered, walks by himself. He gets to his favorite intersection and <u>sees Summer walking towards him</u>. As she gets closer he sees it's not her after all and breathes a sigh of relief.

119A EXT ANOTHER STREET - DAY   119A

Tom continues walking, passing an electronics store. Thinks he sees <u>Summer on all the TVs</u>. He continues to walk.

119B EXT BUS STOP - DAY   119B

Tom gets on a bus.

119C INT. BUS - SAME   119C

Tom sees <u>every passenger on it is Summer</u>. Tom really misses her.

(345)

120   INT. HOTEL FIGUEROA BAR - NIGHT   120

Tom sits alone at the bar. He drinks vodka, waiting for something. And pretty soon, something arrives.

                              ALISON
                    Excuse me? Are you Tom?

                    TOM
          Alison?

Her name is ALISON, red hair, full-figured, not bad looking at all.

                    ALISON
          Yeah. Phew! I was afraid you were
          that guy.

                    TOM
          Nope. Hope you're not disappointed.

                    ALISON
          No. This is much better.

                    TOM
          Yeah totally. So, uh, shall we?

Tom grabs his coat, is about to walk out with her, but swigs what's left of his drink before he does. Tom puts on a brave face and they walk out into:

121   EXT DOWNTOWN STREET - NIGHT   121

Tom and Alison walk down the street, heading for a different restaurant.

                    ALISON
          I normally don't do blind dates but
          Paul and Robyn spoke very highly of
          you. They said you write greeting
          cards. That's so interesting. I
          wanted to write. I majored in
          English at college but... what are
          you gonna do with that degree, you
          know? I went to Brown. Where did --

Tom stops in his tracks, right outside the diner.

                    TOM
          Alison?

                    ALISON
          Hmm?

                    TOM
          Listen... It's great to meet you,
          really. You're a very attractive
          girl. But I should tell you right
          off the bat... this is not going
          anywhere.

                    ALISON
          Oh.

                    TOM
          It's not you. It's me. You seem
          like a real sweet girl and I, just,
          I don't want you to get hurt. You
          know what I mean?

                    ALISON
          Um...

                    TOM
          I know we just met like 3 minutes
          ago but you're probably looking for
          someone to get serious with,
          someone with potential... someone
          who will take you out to eat a few
          times, see a movie, fool around a
          little bit, next thing you know
          you're we're getting a dog and
          you're moving in. And that's not
          me. You want to come inside, have
          some chicken fingers... awesome.
          But that other stuff... I gotta
          tell you up front... I'm just not
          ready, Alison.

Alison can't believe this guy. Tom holds the door open for
Alison. Does she dare go in or does she run away now?

                    ALISON
              (fuck it)
          Chicken fingers sound fine.

122   INT DOWNTOWN DINER RESTAURANT - LATER   122

Tom and Alison, believe it or not, are now eating. There are
three empty shot glasses in front of Tom, one empty bottle of
beer in front of Alison. Tom is feeling the effects.

                    TOM
          Maybe it's uncool to say. But, you
          know what, screw it. I have
          feelings. Does that make me a
          woman? Hell no. I cried in Jerry
          Maguire. That's me, that's who I
          am.

Alison, listening politely, takes a very large gulp of her
beer.

ALISON
Waiter!

She signals for one more drink.

TOM
I liked this girl. Loved her even. And what did she do? She took a giant shit on my face. Literally.

ALISON
Literally?

TOM
(beat)
Not literally. Jesus, that's disgusting, what's wrong with you? The point is I'm messed up. On one hand, I want to forget her. On the other, I think she's the only person on Earth who can make me happy.

ALISON
Uh-huh.

TOM
Every time I think I'm over the hump, I'll have a dream or I'll see some girl who looks like her from the back. And that's it. Back to square one. And you know what...

ALISON
(waits to see if it's
 rhetorical; it isn't)
What?

TOM
I'm gonna get her back. You'll see.

ALISON
Oh will I?

TOM
Absolutely. I think the key is for me to figure out what went wrong. Do you ever do this? Go back and think about all the things you did together. Everything that happened. Replay it over again in your mind, looking for that first sign of trouble.

                    ALISON
            Sure.

                    TOM
            For example...

QUICK CUTS:

123   EXT ANGELUS PLAZA - (BACK ON DAY 95)   123

        Summer and Tom sit in the park looking at buildings. Tom
        writes on summers forearm. Summer looks directly at the
        camera with a face that says "help me god."

124   INT TOM'S BEDROOM - NIGHT - (FROM DAY 31)   124

        From the scene in which Tom and Summer first slept together.
        He's sleeping like a baby, probably the best sleep he's had
        in a long while. Summer lies next to him. Wide awake.
        Unfulfilled.

125   INT ELEVATOR - DAY - (FROM DAY 22)   125

        Tom and Summer ride in silence for a few beats.

                    SUMMER (V.O.)
            Please don't talk to me. Please
            don't talk to me.

                    TOM
            How was your weekend?

126   INT DINER - SAME   126

                    TOM
            Two options really. Either she's an
            evil, emotionless miserable human
            being. Or she's a robot. Vicki from
            "Small Wonder." Would explain a
            lot, actually.

                    ALISON
            Can I ask you a question?

                    TOM
            Shoot.

                    ALISON
            She never cheated on you?

                    TOM
            No! Never.

                    ALISON
          She ever steal or take advantage of
          you in some way?

                    TOM
          Not... really.

                    ALISON
          And she told you up front she
          didn't want a relationship?

                    TOM
          Well... yeah.

                    ALISON
          Jesus Tom... Did she break your
          heart or did you?

They're silent for a few beats. Tom downs the rest of his vodka.

                    TOM
          I got a great idea!

127   INT KARAOKE BAR - LATER   127

Tom is, yes, on stage singing "Train in Vain" by The Clash. The song is usually quite peppy but Tom's version is a cross between Henry Rollins and Alice Cooper. He is losing his fucking mind!

Alison sits by herself in a booth trying to hide her face, having the worst date ever.

(360)

128   EXT - UNION STATION TRAIN PLATFORM - DAY   128

Tom runs to catch a departing train, bound for San Diego. He has a backpack and is carrying a suit and tie on hangers. He runs:

129   INT TRAIN - SAME   129

And starts walking through it. He's looking for someone. Doesn't see him or her. Takes out his cell.

130   SPLITSCREEN w/ McKenzie, in Pacman Cafe.   130

                    TOM
          You here?

                    MCKENZIE
          Hell no.

                    TOM
          What do you mean hell no?

                    MCKENZIE
          I'm not going to that.

                    TOM
          Yes you are.

                    MCKENZIE
          It's gonna be all old people.

                    TOM
          I know! You said you were going.
          That's why I'm going.

The train starts moving.

                    MCKENZIE
          I left a message last night, said I
          was sick. Like a Ninja.

                    TOM
          Dude, now I won't know anyone at
          this thing.

                    MCKENZIE
          Maybe you'll meet a hot
          granddaughter or something.

                    TOM
          I'm hanging up now.

He does. Tom continues to look for a seat. He's looking for two together so he can at least lounge but so far most doubles are taken. He moves into:

131   INT TRAIN CAR #2 - SAME   131

Tom continues to look for a seat. So far nothing. Tom walks by one seat and sees Summer listening to her headphones. He keeps walking.

ANGLE ON TOM. Fuck! Did that just happen? Is she really there? He keeps walking. Probably wasn't her. Just his imagination. Yeah. Finds an open seat at the back. Sits down.

Once situated, he slowly peeks back towards what he thought was Summer. She's looking back too! They both turn away at the same time! Tom mouths "shit!" It's totally her!

STILLS

Joseph Gordon-Levitt and Zooey Deschanel as Tom Hansen and Summer Finn.

Summer Finn. Just another girl.

Tom finds new inspiration for his architecture.

Tom interviews in downtown Los Angeles.

Tom and Summer disagree on Ringo Starr.

Karaoke night brings coworkers together.

Tom's expectations clash with reality.

"Sugar Town" as sung by Summer Finn.

Tom rocks "Here Comes Your Man."

New love and a new game discovered in the park.

Tom gets to know Summer in her apartment.

Director Marc Webb with his two stars.

Marc Webb directs a shot on location in downtown L.A.

Tom moves to the seat by the window, hoping that maybe if he can't see her, she can't see him. Quickly grabs a book from his backpack and buries his face in it.

                    SUMMER (O.S.)
          Hi Tom.

                    TOM
               (mock surprise)
          Oh wow, Summer, hey! Must have
          walked right by you.

                    SUMMER
          Yeah.

                    TOM
          Are you going to Millie's?

                    SUMMER
          Yup. You too?
               (he nods, trying not to
                scream)
          I love Millie. She's the sweetest.

                    TOM
          God I totally forgot you knew her.

                    SUMMER
          Yeah. We... worked together all
          that time.

                    TOM
          Right. Yes. I remember now.

Silence. What the hell do you say here?

                    SUMMER
          So...

                    TOM
          I mean...

                    SUMMER
          How you been? I haven't --

                    TOM
          Good. Good.

                    SUMMER
          Good.

                    SUMMER
          You didn't write back when I --

                    TOM
          No. I know. It got crazy. You
          know... Holiday season and all.

                    SUMMER
          Still working for Vance?

                    TOM
          Yeah.

                    SUMMER
          Hmm.

Silence.

                    SUMMER
          I was gonna go get coffee. I don't
          know if you... Looks like you're
          really into that...
               (reading)
          "The Architecture of Happiness."
          Wow. That sounds great. You should
          keep reading, I don't mean to
          bother you --

She stops, realizes she was rambling. Which is why Tom feels
good about saying:

                    TOM
          Yes. Let's get coffee.

132   INT TRAIN - LOUNGE AREA   132

Tom and Summer at the counter. We don't hear what they're
saying over the din of the train. But they're laughing. Both
of them. Like old times.

133   EXT TRAIN STATION - LATER   133

The train stops. Tom and Summer get out. Look around.

                    SUMMER
          The place is right over there.
          Shall we?

134   EXT - BLUFF - WEDDING CEREMONY - LATER   134

GUESTS are taking their seats. Tom, in suit and tie, waits in
the corridor. A few beats later, Summer appears. Off-white
sundress. Headband. Perfect. Tom forgets to breathe.

                    SUMMER
          You look nice.

                    TOM
            Same here. I mean, yeah. I like
            your... thingy.

Standing at the entrance to the room is an USHER who greets
them.

                    USHER
            Bride or groom.

                    TOM
            Neither.

Summer elbows Tom in the side. Tom looks down at his side,
almost surprised by her actions. It's as if we've reset to
the early part of their relationship.

                    SUMMER
            Bride's side.

                    USHER
            Right this way.

Tom follows Summer in to the room. They take their seats.
Soon enough, the giggles begin.

                    SUMMER
                (whispers)
            Penis.

                    TOM
            Stop it!

135 LATER. MILLIE marries her 70-something GROOM. 135

                    MINISTER
            You may kiss the bride.

He does. Deeply. Tom turns to Summer.

                    TOM
            You're telling me you'll never want
            that?

Summer's face is unreadable. She says nothing.

136 EXT WEDDING RECEPTION - LATER 136

And now the party is in full swing. The band plays something
funky. The revelers dance like they're 30 years younger.

ANGLE ON Tom and Summer's table which is the kid's table.
Tom, Summer, and six CHILDREN (ages 5-8). They find this very
amusing.

137   LATER. Summer dances with one of the kids. She keeps her   137
       eyes on Tom the whole time. He shakes his head at her and
       laughs. She smiles. The time machine to their past still
       seems to be working.

138   LATER. The party toasts the bride and groom. Tom and   138
       Summer, by the bandstand, clink glasses and shout along with
       the others.

139   LATER. Tom and Summer at their seats, surrounded by kids. 139
       The Kids are running around the table playing "Duck Duck
       Goose."

                    SUMMER
           You said you liked it!

                    TOM
           That was chicken? I thought it was
           veal!

                    SUMMER
           No it was chicken!

                    TOM
           Jesus.

                    SUMMER
           What else you got?

                    TOM
           Um... you snore like crazy.

                    SUMMER
           I do not!

                    TOM
           Like a jackhammer.

                    SUMMER
           You do too.

                    TOM
           Oh I definitely do.

                    SUMMER
           And what about your feet?

                    TOM
           What about my feet?

                    SUMMER
          Your feet reek.

                    TOM
          That one time.

                    SUMMER
          Always. And in the morning, your
          hair sticks up like this. Totally
          ridiculous.

                    TOM
          You're ridiculous. Your favorite
          Beatle is Ringo.

                    SUMMER
          Damn right.

At which point Tom is "tapped" by one of the kids. He gets up
and chases after him. The kid makes it to his seat. Tom says
"Duck" twice before immediately tapping Summer. Now she
chases him around the table. They're having a great time.

140   LATER. Millie throws the bouquet. Summer catches it. She   140
      shows it to Tom and shrugs.

141   LATER. Tom and Summer are at the bar. They do shots.   141

                    TOM/SUMMER
          1. 2. 3. GO!

                    TOM
          Ahh. Good stuff. You wanna dance?

                    SUMMER
          Sure.

And so they do. The song is slow, Etta James's "At Last"
(which is free to use, by the way). The two of them don't do
much talking but there's a lot of thinking going on. And
then:

                    SUMMER
          I was wondering...

                    TOM
          Hmm?

                    SUMMER
          I might have a party on Friday.
          There's this really nice roof deck
          that no one uses. Would you
          wanna...?

                    TOM
          I'd like that.

And then the song ends. Tom is about to leave.

                    SUMMER
          Don't go.

And then a fast song begins to play.

                    TOM
          No way Jose. I never dance fast.

Summer steps up to him.

                    SUMMER
          That's ok. We'll just keep dancing
          slow.

And so they do. Best wedding ever.

142   INT TRAIN - NIGHT   142

Summer is asleep on Tom's shoulder. Tom is wide awake, looking out the window. He looks over at Summer. Sound asleep. Closer then they've been in months. Looks back out the window, a wan smile on his face. They're gonna make it after all.

                                             CUT TO:

143   CU PAUL, TALKING DIRECTLY TO THE CAMERA DOCUMENTARY STYLE 143

                    PAUL
          I just got lucky I guess. We met in
          elementary school. We had the same
          class schedule in the 7th grade and
          we just... clicked.

                                             CUT TO:

144   CU MCKENZIE.   144

                    MCKENZIE
          Love? Shit, I don't know. Long as
          she's cute and she's willing,
          right? I'm flexible on the cute.

145   CU RACHEL.   145

                    RACHEL
          That's a pretty complex question.
          Philosophers, poets, scientists,
          everybody has a theory, don't they?
          I kinda like what Nietzsche said:
          "There is always some madness in
          love, but there is also...always
          some reason in madness." Pretty
          smart. Then again, Nietzsche went
          crazy from syphillis. So there's
          that.

146   CU VANCE.   146

                    VANCE.
          I've been happily married for 30
          years. She's the light that guides
          me home.
                    (beat)
          Yes it *is* from one of our cards.
                    (beat)
          No someone else wrote it. Doesn't
          make it less true.

147   CU Millie   147

                    MILLIE
          I was very much in love with my
          first husband. And it was the
          unhappiest decade of my life.

148   CU SUMMER   148

                    SUMMER
          I think my feelings on this subject
          have already been covered. Can we
          please talk about something else
          for a change?

149   CU MILLIE'S GROOM   149

                    MILLIE'S GROOM
          41 years is a long time to wait for
          the right person. I was starting to
          wonder if I'd ever find her.
                    (thinks of something and
                     smiles)
          41 years... It was worth the wait.

150   CU PAUL   150

                         PAUL
            I wouldn't say "the girl of my
            dreams," no. The girl of my dreams
            would have a better rack. Probably
            different hair, could like sports a
            little more. But... truth is...
            Robyn's better than the girl of my
            dreams... She's real.

151   CU TOM. He says nothing. Just stands there. Still trying   151
      to figure things out. Off his look, we cut to:

152   ANIMATION. A QUICK recap of the earlier color sequence.   152

      A song begins. Slow and steady but it'll build as we CUT TO:

(366)

153   EXT SUMMER'S APARTMENT BUILDING - DUSK   153

      The song continues to play. Gift in hand, Tom stands at the
      foot of a four-story walk-up building, looking up at the
      roof, which is wrapped by a halo of white Xmas lights. It's
      already bustling with activity.

      He's going up. As he does, <u>the screen splits</u>.

154   <u>On the left</u>, we see Tom going upstairs. This side is   154
      labeled "**Reality**."

      <u>On the right</u>, we also see Tom going upstairs. This side is
      labeled "**Expectations**." There the same image for a beat.

155   INT SUMMER'S APARTMENT - SAME   155

      But then "**Expectations**" arrives first. Summer invites Tom
      inside. She gives him a huge embrace. She kisses him, right
      where the lips meet the cheek. Very close to a full-frontal
      lip kiss. (ECU the point of kiss contact).

      "**Reality**" arrives soon after. She comes over and gives him a
      huge embrace. She kisses him, but her kiss lands firmly in
      cheekville. (ECU the point of kiss contact).

      Both Toms give both Summers the book as a gift. It's
      "Architecture of Happiness." Both Summers accept it eagerly.

156   EXT ROOF - SAME   156

      <u>On the right</u>, Summer introduces "**Expectations**" to three
      or four guests.

The whole party is maybe six people total and Summer takes "**Expectations**" Tom to the side so they can be alone.

<u>On the left</u>, Summer introduces "**Reality**" to a circle of seven or eight people. (NOTE: This is the scene we saw on p. 51-52). The party is actually quite large, with 30 or 40 people Tom has never seen before in his life. Summer's friends, without him.

157 While "**Expectations**" and Summer continue to talk intimately, Summer leaves "**Reality**" alone as she flits around the roof. Tom gets a drink. Smiles at a cute girl but has no interest. Minds his business waiting for Summer's return.

<u>On the right</u>, "**Expectations**" and Summer remain locked in a serious conversation. They don't take their eyes off one another. Summer plays with her hair. Their knees are almost touching.

<u>On the left</u>, "**Reality**" continues to stand by himself. He takes in the scene. Who are all these people? He looks around for Summer but doesn't see her anywhere. Still optimistic.

<u>On the right</u>, Summer grabs "**Expectations**" and pulls him away from the rest of the party. They're all over each other.

158 <u>On the left</u>, "**Reality**" Tom looks out over the city. Tom wants to tell Summer about this. Looks for her again on the roof.

And then he sees her. While "**Expectations**" and Summer are locked in some passionate embrace, "**Reality**" sees Summer do something odd. She's showing some FEMALE FRIENDS a ring on her finger. An engagement ring. (Yes, she's been wearing it the whole time.)

Tom doesn't process this at first. He takes a step, still planning to tell her about her view, before realizing the significance of what he's seeing. Then he stops in his tracks.

Summer sees Tom and puts it all together. Her face drops. She pulls her hand away from her friends and walks over to him.

               SUMMER
          It just happened!

And he just races past her before she can stop him. The music builds...

158A INT SUMMER'S APARTMENT - SAME   158A

Summer pulls "**Expectations**" into her apartment and shuts the door. They fall onto the bed. <u>END SPLITSCREEN</u>.

| 159 | INT STAIRWELL - SAME | 159 |

"**Reality**" Tom comes running down the stairs and exits the building.

| 160 | EXT SUMMER'S APARTMENT BUILDING - SAME | 160 |

Tom storms out of the building.

| 160A | INT SUMMER'S APARTMENT - SAME | 160A |

Summer calls after him from her apartment doorway.

                    SUMMER
          Tom!?

But he's gone.

| 160B | EXT STREET - SAME | 160B |

Tom, away from her building. As he does, his entire universe falls apart. FX: All around Tom, Summer's building and then the entire city is COMPLETELY ERASED, brick by brick, beam by beam, as if by an unseen force. Tom's world is reduced to nothing. END MUSIC.

(402)

| 161 | INT TOM'S BEDROOM | 161 |

The half-destroyed alarm clock goes off. Tom hits the off button.

(403)

| 162 | INT TOM'S BEDROOM | 162 |

Same exact thing.

(403 1/2)

| 163 | INT SUPERMARKET - DAY | 163 |

Tom, in a robe and boxer shorts, buys milk, OJ, cigarettes, Jack Daniels, and twinkies.

The CLERK eyes him suspiciously.

| 164 | EXT STREET - SAME | 164 |

Tom sees a COUPLE kissing on the sidewalk. He snaps.

          TOM
Get a room!

They look at this lunatic in his robe and quickly walk away.

(404)

| 165 | INT TOM'S BEDROOM | 165 |

Alarm clock. We PAN ACROSS to see Tom is wide awake. He probably hasn't slept in a day or so. He has no reaction to the alarm.

| 166 | INT OFFICE - LATER | 166 |

Tom actually wanders in to work, wearing sunglasses and the clothes he slept in. People pass and say hello. He can't muster responses. At his desk:

          MCKENZIE
I've been calling every five minutes. Are you ok?

          TOM
Great.

          MCKENZIE
What happened to you?

          TOM
Don't want to talk about it.

          MCKENZIE
You always want to talk about it.

          TOM
Not this.

          MCKENZIE
Well come on let's go.

          TOM
Where we going?

          MCKENZIE
It's _Thursday_!

167   INT BOARDROOM - LATER   167

Tom sits next to McKenzie and across from Vance. He's in his usual boardroom position, which is to say, near comatose.

A female CO-WORKER, 50s, stands at the front of the room in mid-presentation, showing slides that have something to do with a cat in various poses. First we see, "Cat Reaching Up for Out-of-Reach Milk Bowl."

>   CO-WORKER
> This one says "Go for it!"

Click. We see "Cat Considering a Giant Leap."

>   CO-WORKER
> And this one says "You can do it!"
> We have a whole line of
> inspirational cards featuring
> Pickles, my cat. I think people
> will really enjoy them. Thank you.

She takes her seat.

>   VANCE.
> Good job Rhoda. Inspirational
> stuff. Now, who's next? We haven't
> heard from "Sympathy" in a while.
> Hansen...

>   TOM
>   (reacting to his name)
> Hmm?

>   VANCE.
> The Winter collection. You have
> anything to contribute?

>   TOM
> Uh...no. I really don't.

>   VANCE.
>   (disappointed)
> Oh...k. We'll come back to you.
> McKenzie --

>   TOM
> You know what...?

>   VANCE.
> Yes Tom.

                    TOM
          Can I say something about the cat?

                    VANCE
          Well sure. Go ahead.

                    TOM
          This here is, and Rhoda, you know I
          mean no disrespect... but this...
          this is total shit.

                    MCKENZIE
          Tom!

                    TOM
          "You can do it?" "Go for it?"

He points to the screen, still showing the "Cat About to
Leap" image.

                    TOM
          That's not inspirational. It's
          suicidal. Pickles tries to go for
          it right there, that's a dead cat.
          No, this is all lies. We're <u>liars</u>!
          I mean, think about it... why do
          people buy these things? Not to say
          how they feel. People buy these
          cards when they <u>can't</u> say how they
          feel. Or they're afraid to. And we
          provide the service that lets 'em
          off the hook!

Tom is getting excited. The rest of the room is growing
uncomfortable.

                    TOM
          You know what... I say to hell with
          it! Let's level with America. Or at
          least make them speak for
          themselves! I mean, seriously,
          what's this...
              (picks a card off the
               table)
          "Congratulations on your new baby."
          Eh... How bout... "Congratulations
          on your new baby... Guess that's it
          for hanging out. Nice knowing ya."

                    VANCE
          Hansen, please sit --

                    TOM
               (picks up a card)
          Oh wait, what's this? Ooh look at
          all the pretty hearts. Let's open
          it up. "Happy Valentine's Day,
          Sweetheart. I love you." Oh that's
          nice. Aint love grand?
               (beat)
          See this is what I'm talking about.
          What's that even mean, "love?" Do
          you know? Do you? Does anyone?

                    MCKENZIE
               (sensing a meltdown)
          Tom...

                    TOM
          If someone gave me this card, Mr.
          Vance... I would eat it.

Tom sits down on the desk, defeated.

                    TOM
          It's these cards and these movies
          and these pop songs. They're to
          blame for all the lies, the
          heartache, everything! We're
          responsible!
               (beat)
          I'm responsible.

Everyone shifts in their seats.

                    TOM
          I think we do a bad thing here.
          People should be able to say how
          they feel, how they really feel,
          without some strangers putting
          words in their mouths. Words like
          "love" that don't mean shit.

Tom gets up and walks to the door.

                    TOM
          I'm sorry Mr. Vance, but I quit.
          There's enough bullshit in the
          world without my help.

With that, Tom gets up and walks out of the room. Everyone is
pretty stunned. Someone coughs. McKenzie tries to start a
clap. It doesn't really take.

                                             CUT TO:

168   EXT BUILDING - MINUTES LATER   168

Tom exits the building onto the downtown street. He stands there for a beat. Shit. Now what?

                                                    CUT TO:

(419)

169   EXT FIELD - DAY   169

Tom watches Rachel playing soccer. He has a notebook on his lap and is sketching with a pencil. We hear a whistle and Rachel comes back to the bench.

                    RACHEL
            You're sketching again!

                    TOM
            Just doodling.

                    RACHEL
            We got 20 seconds. Talk to me. You
            ok?

                    TOM
            Me? I'm good. I'm great.

Rachel looks at Tom's notebook. He's sketched a flip book of himself being stabbed repeatedly by a pitchfork-wielding Summer (complete with devil horns).

                    RACHEL
            Riiight.

Tom hides the book behind his back.

                    RACHEL
            You know, my friends are all in
            love with you.

He sees a coven of 13-year olds eyeing him from the sidelines.

                    RACHEL
            Like we said, plenty other fish in
            the sea.

                    TOM
            Thanks Rach but those are guppies.

The whistle blows again. Rachel gets ready to go back. But before she does:

                    RACHEL
Tom.

                    TOM
Hmm?

                    RACHEL
I know you think she was "the one."
      (beat)
I don't. I think you're just remembering the good stuff. Next time you look back, you should look again.

She blows him a kiss and then runs back onto the field. Tom watches her go. Off his face, we cut to:

(240)

170   EXT ANGELUS PLAZA - DAY   170

Tom and Summer are having the picnic we saw on page 5. This is that fateful day Tom described to his sister and his friends. The day it all, finally, fell apart.

They eat in silence on the bench. Summer is hardly even looking at him. Tom tries to make eye contact. Hmm. Is something in the air? We stay with them for a few extra beats of silence.

171   EXT DOWNTOWN FOOD MARKET - LATER   171

Tom and Summer shopping at the fruit market. Unless we were looking for trouble we wouldn't see any. But since we are, we might notice she lags behind him as they walk through the aisles. His hands are in his pockets. She's distant. But only if we're really looking.

172   INT COFFEE HOUSE - LATER   172

That day again. As we've seen before, Tom reads a newspaper. Summer reads a novel.

                    TOM
It's playing at 5.

                    SUMMER
You want to go?

                    TOM
          I don't know. You wanna maybe go
          back to your place or ---

                    SUMMER
          I want to see it. Let's go.

                    TOM
          Ok cool.

                    SUMMER
          Unless you don't want to.

                    TOM
          No, I will. That's fine.

                    SUMMER
          Ok.

     A few more silent beats. Something's in the air.

173 INT MOVIE - LATER   173

     Tom and Summer watching the film. Tears begin to well in
     Summer's eyes. They soon turn to audible sobs. Tom turns to
     look at her, to offer some sort of comfort, believing it to
     be a response to the movie. She doesn't look back.

174 EXT MOVIE THEATRE - LATER   174

     Same day from the past. They walk out, at first everything's
     alright. It's exactly as we saw on page 5. But soon after
     that she begins to cry again. Serious, real sobbing.

                    TOM
          Hey.

     He goes to hug her. He hugs her. It's unclear if she hugs
     back.

                    TOM
          Hey Sum, it's just a movie.

                    SUMMER
          I know. I'm sorry.

                    TOM
          What's the matter?

                    SUMMER
          It's nothing. I'm being ridiculous.

                    TOM
               (not sure)
          Ok.

They continue on.

175   INT RECORD STORE - LATER   175

Tom and a much more in control Summer walk down the aisles.
He grabs a record.

                    TOM
          It pains me that we live in a world
          where no one's ever heard of
          Spearmint.

                    SUMMER
          I've never heard of them.

                    TOM
          They're on that disc I made you.
               (beat)
          They're Track 1.

                    SUMMER
          Oh.

Tom shakes that off, grabs a Ringo Starr album and shows it
to her, just as we've seen in the beginning. She smiles and
they continue on down the aisles.

In CU, Tom goes to hold Summer's hand. But something happens.
It could be a total coincidence, but just as his hand
approaches hers (in SLO-MO), she moves it away and keeps it
at her side. Tom puts his hands in his pockets, unsure if
there's something to read in that.

176   EXT RECORD STORE - LATER   176

Again, that fateful day continues. Tom and Summer outside.

                    SUMMER
          So.

                    TOM
          So... Now what? You hungry? Wanna
          get some dinner or something?

                    SUMMER
          I think I'm gonna call it a day.

                    TOM
          You sure?

                    SUMMER
          Yeah. I've got pasta at home.

                    TOM
               (beat)
          Hey Sum... Is everything alright
          with you?

                    SUMMER
          Yeah. I'm just tired.

                    TOM
          If something's bothering you... you
          can talk you me. You know that
          right?

                    SUMMER
          I know.

                    TOM
          I'm here for you. I just wish you'd
          let me in.

Summer looks at him sadly. And she kisses him gently on the
cheek. It's a real weird move for her. Tom isn't sure what it
means. There's an awkward silence which Tom becomes desperate
to break.

                    TOM
               (eureka!)
          I got it!
               (off her look)
          Pancakes.

And the rest as they say is history.

CUE UP MUSIC which plays over:

(421-464)

177	MONTAGE: TOM GETS HIS SHIT TOGETHER. MAYBE.	177
177A	INT TOM'S BEDROOM - DAY	177A

Tom sits in his bed, angrily throwing a tennis ball against
the wall. Rolls off his bed, lies face first on the ground
eating the carpet. Has he given up?

No.

Slowly, Tom lifts himself off the ground. Does a push-up. Then another.

| 178 | OMITTED | 178 |

| 179 | INT TOM'S BEDROOM - LATER | 179 |

Tom erases all the greeting card paraphernalia from the chalkboard above his bed. Looks at the empty board for a beat.

| 180 | OMITTED | 180 |

| 181 | INT TOM'S APARTMENT - LATER | 181 |

Tom sits with his feet up on a table, headphones on his ears, reading one of many Taschen books on innovative building design.

| 181A | INT TOM'S BEDROOM - LATER | 181A |

We now see a list of names on the chalkboard. These are architecture firms. Tom has a phone in one hand, is sketching something new with the other.

| 182 | INT OFFICE LOBBY - DAY | 182 |

Tom drops off his portfolio with the security guard in the lobby of a high-rise.

| 183 | INSERT: CU HANDS lacing the back of a dress. | 183 |

| 184 | INT - KITCHEN - NIGHT | 184 |

Tom, Rachel, Mom and Step-dad eat dinner as a family.

| 185 | INSERT: CU HANDS tending to the train of the dress. | 185 |

| 186 | INT TOM'S BEDROOM - DAY | 186 |

Tom getting bad news on the phone. He crosses a name off the list. We notice several others are also crossed off. We also notice a pretty impressive sketch now on the chalkboard.

| 187 | INSERT: CU VEIL coming down over a face. | 187 |

| 187A | EXT TOM'S ROOFTOP - DAY | 187A |

Tom sketches the cityscape from his rooftop. He has his mojo back in a big way.

| 188 | INT TOM'S BEDROOM - NIGHT | 188 |

Tom getting more bad news from the answering machine, crossing off yet another firm from the list. Few remain. He sits on the bed with his shoulders slumped. For a beat, lost in thought. Then, as if to shut those thoughts out, whatever they were, he goes back to the chalkboard and continues his sketch.

SPLITSCREEN - DAY

189 <u>On the LEFT</u>, Tom, alone, on a bus. Looking out the window. Thinking.

190 <u>On the RIGHT</u>, Summer. In the wedding dress. The veil is lifted. And she's a bride.

END MUSIC.

(488)

191 EXT OFFICE BUILDING - ANOTHER DAY

Tom, in a suit, exits a building after another dismal interview. We can see he is frustrated but not deterred. In the distance, his favorite spot in the city, where he took Summer ages ago.

192 EXT. ANGELUS PLAZA - DAY

Tom walks over and sits down on that bench, his favorite. He stares off, lost in thought. And then, from out of nowhere, there's her voice.

> SUMMER (V.O.)
> Hey.

Summer sits like an apparition on a neighboring bench. She may have just sat down, she may have been there for hours. Tom isn't sure if she's real or what to do.

> SUMMER
> I always loved this place, ever since you brought me.

> TOM
> What's not to like?

Awkward silence.

> TOM
> So... I should probably say congratulations.

                    SUMMER
          Only if you mean it.

                    TOM
          In that case...

He doesn't say anything. This makes her smile.

                    SUMMER
          So... you're ok?

                    TOM
          I will be. Eventually.

                    SUMMER
          Well that's good.

                    TOM
          Yeah I quit the office.

                    SUMMER
               (surprised)
          No kidding? That's... That's great
          Tom. Really.

Awkward silence.

                    TOM
          And you're married.

                    SUMMER
          Crazy, huh?

More awkward silence. This one goes on a beat longer. And then:

                    TOM
          You should have said something.

                    SUMMER
          I know.

                    TOM
          At the wedding. When we were
          dancing.

                    SUMMER
          He hadn't asked me yet.

                    TOM
          But he was in your life.

                    SUMMER
          Yeah.

                    TOM
          Why'd you dance with me?

                    SUMMER
          I wanted to.

                    TOM
          You do what you want, don't you?

Summer genuinely does feel bad about all this.

                    TOM
          You never wanted to be anyone's
          "girlfriend" and now you're...
          somebody's wife.

                    SUMMER
          Surprised me too.

                    TOM
              (sighs)
          I don't think I'll ever understand
          that.

                    SUMMER
          Tom --

                    TOM
          No, seriously, I mean, it doesn't
          make sense.

                    SUMMER
          It just happened.

                    TOM
          But that's what I don't understand.
          What just happened?

                    SUMMER
          I... Tom... I just... I woke up one
          day and I knew...

                    TOM
          Knew what?

                    SUMMER
          What I was never sure of with you.

And there's not much else to say after that.

>   TOM
> I'll tell you what sucks, Summer.
> Realizing that everything you
> believe in is complete and utter
> bullshit. That sucks.
>
>   SUMMER
> What do you mean?
>
>   TOM
> Destiny, soulmates, true love. All
> that stuff. Silly childhood fairy
> tale nonsense. I should have
> listened to you. You were right all
> along.

Summer takes a beat to let this hang there.

>   SUMMER
> I was right?

And then, out of nowhere, she begins to hysterically laugh.

>   TOM
> What? This is funny?

Tries to stop but it only makes it worse. Now's she's completely cracking up.

>   TOM
> What are you laughing at?

And she can't stop. She's totally lost control.

>   TOM
>   (trying himself not to
>   laugh)
> You're a crazy person!
>
>   SUMMER
> You're the crazy person!
>
>   TOM
> What are you talking about?!
>
>   SUMMER
> One day I'm reading "Dorian Gray"
> at the corner deli and this guy
> sits down and starts asking about
> it. Now he's my husband!
>
>   TOM
> This is funny to you?

                    SUMMER
          What would have happened if I went
          to the movies instead? If I went
          somewhere else for lunch? If I
          showed up at the very same spot
          just ten minutes later? Tom, it was
          meant to be, just like you said.
          And as it was happening, I knew it.
          I could feel it. And I kept
          thinking to myself "Wow. Tom was
          right." You were right about all of
          it.
              (beat)
          It just wasn't *me* you were right
          about.

Tom is speechless. Summer takes his hand. We may notice her wedding ring. We may also notice that this is the same exact shot as the first scene. We hold it for a few seconds more. And then, the hands separate.

                    SUMMER
          Anyway, I should probably be
          getting back. It was good to see
          you. I'm glad you're well.

Summer gets up and starts walking away from him. ANGLE on Tom, watching her go.

                    TOM
          Summer!

She stops and turns back. He takes in her face, most likely for the last time ever.

                    TOM
          I really *do* hope you're happy.

                    SUMMER
              (beat)
          I know.

And she smiles and walks away. The CAMERA TRACKS AWAY with her, leaving Tom alone in the park. He gets smaller and farther away with every second.

                                        FADE OUT.

A FEW SECONDS OF BLACK.

> NARRATOR (V.O.)
> If Tom had learned anything... it was that you shouldn't ascribe great cosmic significance to a simple earthly event.

AND THEN WE FADE
THE FUCK BACK
IN:

(500)

193 INT OFFICE WAITING AREA - DAY 193

Tom, in a suit, with a hefty batch of architecture sketches at his side, waits in the foyer of Allen, Prince, and Gethers Architecture, a cool indie firm in the city that operates out of the 4th floor of the famous Bradbury Building on 3rd and Broadway.

Tom waits. We will notice, before he does, a VERY CUTE GIRL sitting in a another chair, also waiting. They see one another. She smiles. He smiles back.

> GIRL
> Are you here to interview?

> TOM
> Sorry?

> GIRL
> Are you interviewing? For the position?

> TOM
> Oh. Yeah. Why, are you?

> GIRL
> Yup.

> TOM
> Ah. My competition.

> GIRL
> It would appear.

> TOM
> So, uh, little awkward.

                    GIRL
          Yeah.

                    TOM
          Well, I hope you... don't get the
          job.

                    GIRL
          I hope you don't get the job.

They both laugh. There's a silence for a few beats. And it's
during this time that something weird comes over Tom and we
can visibly see it in his face. He likes the look of this
girl. This girl is cute. He'd like to talk more with her.
And, he's a little surprised by it.

                    TOM
          So, uh...

                    GIRL
          Hmm?

                    TOM
          Are you from...California?

                    GIRL
          Grew up not too far from here.
          Atherton, near Stanford.

                    TOM
          Yeah I know Atherton. Nice area.

                    GIRL
          Have I seen you before?

                    TOM
          I, uh, I don't think so.

                    GIRL
          Do you ever go to Angelus Plaza?

                    TOM
          I love it there. It's like my
          favorite spot in the city.

                    GIRL
          Right. Except for the parking lots.

                    TOM
          Yes! Exactly. I totally agree!

                    GIRL
          Uh-huh. I think I've seen you
          there.

                    TOM
          Huh. I've never seen you.

                    GIRL
          You must not have been looking.

Tom ponders this a beat.

                    NARRATOR
          Coincidence. That's all anything
          ever is. Nothing more than
          coincidence.

A MAN comes out.

                    MAN
          Tom Hansen?

                    TOM
          Yes.

                    MAN
          Come on back.

                    TOM
          Thank you.

He starts to go. But halfway through the doorway, he pauses
and looks back at the girl.

194   ANIMATION. 1 second clip of the colored sequence. Real   194
      fast. Hardly noticeable. But it's there.

195   NARRATOR   195
          It took a long time but Tom had
          finally learned. There are no
          miracles. There's no such thing as
          <u>fate</u>. Nothing is meant to be. He
          knew. He was sure of it now.
                (beat)
          Tom was...

Tom turns back around.

                    NARRATOR
          ...he was pretty sure.

                    TOM
               (to Girl)
          Excuse me.

                    GIRL
          You again.

                    TOM
          When this is over... would you like
          to maybe...grab a cup of coffee or
          something?

                    GIRL
          Oh. I'm sorry. I'm sorta supposed
          to meet someone.

                    TOM
               (deflated)
          Got it... No problem.

He turns back around and shakes that off, tries to refocus on
the task at hand. A job interview. And then he hears.

                    GIRL
          Sure.

Tom turns back around.

                    TOM
          What's that?

                    GIRL
          Why not?

                    TOM
          Yeah?

                    GIRL
          Yeah.

                    TOM
          Great! So... I'll wait for you
          here, or you wait for me
          or...something.

She laughs. She's cute when she laughs.

                    GIRL
          We'll figure it out.

                    TOM
          Ok!
               (extends hand to shake)
          My name's Tom.

                    GIRL
          Nice to meet you...

She puts out her hand to meet his. They shake.

                    GIRL
          I'm Autumn.

And on his face...

                                        SMASH CUT TO:

(1)

THE END.

PRODUCTION NOTES

"I think the key is for me to figure out what went wrong. Do you ever do this? Go back and think about all the things you did together. Everything that happened. Replay it over again in your mind, looking for the first sign of trouble."

— Tom

This is a story of boy meets girl, begins the wry, probing narrator of *500 Days of Summer*, and with that the film takes off at breakneck speed into a funny, true-to-life and unique dissection of the unruly and unpredictable year and a half of one young man's no-holds-barred love affair.

Tom, the boy, still believes, even in this cynical modern world, in the notion of a transforming, cosmically destined, lightning-strikes-once kind of love. Summer, the girl, doesn't. Not at all. But that doesn't stop Tom from going after her, again and again, like a modern Don Quixote, with all his might and courage. Suddenly, Tom is in love not just with a lovely, witty, intelligent woman – *not that he minds any of that* — but with the very *idea* of Summer, the very idea of a love that still has the power to shock the heart and stop the world.

The fuse is lit on Day 1 – when Tom (Joseph Gordon-Levitt), a would-be architect turned sappy greeting card writer encounters Summer (Zooey Deschanel), his boss's breezy, beautiful new secretary, fresh off the plane from Michigan. Though seemingly out of his league, Tom soon discovers he shares plenty in common with Summer. After all, they both love The Smiths. They both have a thing for the surrealist artist Magritte. Tom once lived in Jersey and Summer has a cat named Bruce. As Tom muses, "we're compatible like crazy."

By Day 31, things are moving ahead, albeit "casually." By Day 32, Tom is irreparably smitten, living in a giddy, fantastical world of Summer on his mind. By Day 185, things are in serious limbo — but not without hope. And as the story winds backwards and forwards through Tom and Summer's on-again, off-again, sometimes blissful, often tumultuous dalliance it covers the whole dizzying territory from infatuation, dating and sex to separation, recrimination and redemption in a whirl of time jumps, split screens, karaoke numbers and cinematic verve – all of which adds up to a kaleidoscopic portrait of why, and how, we still struggle so laughably, cringingly hard to make sense of love . . . and to hopefully make it real.

Fox Searchlight Pictures presents *500 Days of Summer*, a Watermark Production, which marks the feature directorial debut of Marc Webb from a script written by Scott Neustadter & Michael H. Weber (*Pink Panther 2*). The producers are Jessica Tuchinsky, Mark Waters, Mason Novick and Steven J. Wolfe. The team who turned the 500 days of Tom and Summer's romance into a cinematic whirlwind of ideas includes director of photography Eric Steelberg (*Juno*), editor Alan Edward Bell (*Little Manhattan, The Comebacks*), production designer Laura Fox (*All God's Children Can Dance*) and Emmy® nominated costume designer Hope Hanafin (*Warm Springs, Lackawanna Blues*).

A Comment From Co-Writer Scott Neustadter

On July 22nd 2001, a Sunday if I'm not mistaken (and I'm not), sometime between the hours of 7 and 9 (Eastern Standard Time), a monumental, cataclysmic, earth-shattering event took place at a restaurant called "Serendipity" in New York – I got dumped... hard. We'd only been dating a couple months and yet, as often happens in the wake of such things, I was flooded by some powerful emotions: hopelessness, crippling inadequacy, the world ending, that sort of thing. I stayed in a lot during those days – listening to the Smiths on a constant loop, watching old French films and lamenting my not being alive in an era that would appreciate me. In short, I was an asshole.

Now at this time, my friend Weber and I had written one screenplay together, an outlandish and rather inane comedy solely designed to make us both laugh. A few people read it and thought it was funny but nothing ever happened and that was that. We kept writing but rarely finished anything we started. And then, after a few aborted attempts to write something big and commercial, my frustration level, coupled with my already gloomy mental state, convinced me that I needed to do something nuts. So I did. I impulsively quit my job of 4 years, said goodbye to my friends and family, and flew off to London for an indefinite period of time (to "study," as I told all those concerned).

An amazing thing happened next. Almost instantly upon my arrival, I met someone new. She was smart. She was pretty. She was perfect. Six months later, she dumped me. *500 Days of Summer* is the story of those relationships. Or, at least, how I remembered them afterwards. (Ok, fine – how I *chose* to remember them.) Weber and I always dreamed of writing a romantic comedy like our heroes Cameron Crowe and Woody Allen – one that was relatable and identifiable, where the comedy came from a real place rather than some squirrel attack in the woods. Our aim was simple – tell the story of a relationship, make it real, make it funny, try to make it not suck.

This is the result. An anatomy of a romance. Equal parts autobiography and fantasy. A pop song in movie form. *500 Days* is a lot of things – funny (hopefully), sad (definitely), peculiar (for sure). There's music and dancing, split screens, narrators and a cartoon bird. The one thing there *isn't* is irony. But today, looking back on the experience, I can indeed find something wholly ironic – that an idea born from the pain of two bad relationships has directly led to some of the best in my life, with a great director, amazing producers, and practically everyone else involved in the project.

The Beginnings of Summer: Penning a Postmodern Love Story

"For all intents and purposes, Summer Finn – just another girl. Except she wasn't."
— The Narrator

500 Days of Summer began in angst. It was sparked by two young screenwriters – one single and recovering from a badly bruised heart, the other in a long-term relationship — reminiscing over romances that could have been, that maybe *should* have been, but somehow just . . . weren't. Almost everyone has had one and, in an age when everything seems to happen faster and more intensely, they seem to be ever more common. So how, wondered Scott Neustadter and Michael Weber, does a young romantic survive such a reality? And how could today's version of romantic idealism be portrayed on the screen in a way it's never really been seen before?

"There are certain topics that romantic comedies always hint around and never really tackle directly," says Neustadter. "Questions such as: is there really such a thing as 'the one?' And, if there is, what happens if you lose her? What do you do now? Can you still believe in love? Do your beliefs about love change? These were the questions Weber and I wanted to write about even though we don't quite have the answers."

Thus was born the character of Tom Hansen, a guy who believes madly, passionately, even unreasonably in the mystery and power of love, and the woman who doesn't – Tom's romantic muse, total obsession and the frustratingly non-committal, destiny-denying bane of his existence: Summer. But it wasn't just Tom that the screenwriters were interested in; it was the inner workings of his *memory*, as he looks back on just what really happened between him and Summer.

"The idea we had for the screenplay was sort of a romantic comedy meets *Memento*. We wanted to follow a guy sifting through the memories of a relationship, moving backwards and forwards through time as he starts to see things he might not have seen while he was going through it," explains Neustadter. "You watch him gaining perspective and learning something about himself and about love. Tom realizes he is someone who is in love with the idea of love and that's why his story becomes a very hopeful one. He sees something about the nature of love. It's not your conventional romantic comedy, but it is a very romantic story."

From the beginning Neustadter and Weber chafed against the perennially cutesy, sentimental and unexamined conventions of romantic comedies — and searched for a truer way to tell Tom's story of the romance that put his heart through a mix-master, only to leave him with an even stronger, if more mature, belief in love. "We threw away all the rules and looked at alternative structures," explains Neustadter. "We followed every single idea no matter how crazy it seemed, from the way people are transported by a song to how they drown their sorrows in a movie. Anything that was in Tom's mind and memory was fair game."

Continues Weber: "Writing this movie became an incredibly creative experience, because we gave ourselves so much freedom and we were constantly exploring how people's emotions and relationships are tied up in the culture all around us — in the songs, movies, books, television and art by which we define our identities."

Neustadter and Weber also freely played with time, moving ahead and then back-pedaling through Tom and Summer's relationship at will. "Jumbling the chronology of the movie was a lot of fun for us," continues Weber, "but there was also a method to our madness. By pulling out certain moments on their way up and on their way down, you see things you might not otherwise notice and from a new persepective. And, if you think about it, that's how memory really works, where something will trigger your mind to think of an amazing, wonderful moment and then that will trigger the memory of a bad moment and then comes a revelation of how they were all connected."

Most of all, the priority was on keeping the whole process as emotionally honest as the two men could possibly withstand. "We've all been in the trenches of love, we've all gone through the highs and lows, so Scott and I felt that the only way to tell this story was to come at it from a completely real place," says Weber. "It was pretty interesting for us because Scott was just going through a break-up and I was in a long-term, stable relationship, so we each brought a totally opposite perspective, living it and not living it, and I think that tension helped to bring out more of the comedy."

Ultimately it was that thread of emotional honesty that drew a diverse team of talent to *500 Days of Summer*. Says producer Mason Novick, who also produced last year's unconventional and widely acclaimed hit comedy *Juno*: "This is a story that doesn't fit directly into any genre or label. It's not your typical romantic comedy and it's not your typical drama – it's an intriguing, funny, fresh perspective on what modern relationships are really like. And it attracted just the right group of people to pull it all together."

Novick was amazed to learn just how much of the playful, fast-paced screenplay was pulled straight from real life. "Of course, truth is often stranger than fiction," he says. "Some of the scenes I thought had to have been imagined the writers told me, 'no, no, that really happened.' They were able to bring that quality of reality and put it together with their very unique view of the world and of becoming part of a couple."

Adds producer Jessica Tuchinsky, who is partnered with producer Mark Waters (director of such films as *Freaky Friday, Mean Girls* and *The Spiderwick Chronicles*) in Watermark Pictures: "The two writers, Scott and Michael, are basically two Toms. They've grown up on the same songs, the same movies and they've felt the same fireworks when they've fallen in love as Tom in the movie and they put all of that into the script in a very clever way structurally."

Producer Steven Wolfe (who brought the iconoclastic Polish Brothers to the fore with their directorial debut, *Twin Falls, Idaho*) notes that everyone who read the script realized it would need a very special touch: "It uses a multitude of storytelling devices, and it's very complex in how it flashes backwards and forwards and uses these total fantasy moments and pulls all these different pieces together into a puzzle," he says. "We knew it would need a director who could plan everything right down to the most minute detail."

The search for a director with a vision that could stand up to the screenplay's creativity led the filmmaking team to newcomer Marc Webb, who had cut his teeth on music videos and commercials and was in search of his first feature film. He quickly gave his own heart to *500 Days of Summer*. "When I first read the script, it was like Tom seeing Summer for the first time," muses Webb. "Something clicked and I just knew this was the one."

Like any man infatuated, it was a sense of mystery that drew him deeper in. "The first time I read it, I remember feeling something I couldn't define," Webb recalls. "When I went back and read it again, I realized there is a theme in the movie that is implicit, it's not ever explicitly stated, but it's that Tom finally is hit with the idea that happiness is found within. He sees that it isn't in the big blue of eyes of the girl in the cubicle down the hall, even though she can be very beguiling and gets him thinking that she is what will bring him happiness. The truth is that you have to realize who you are and understand your own potential before you can really find true love. At the end of the day I felt this story was a very fun way to say something that had some meaning for me."

Webb was also excited about the daring style of *500 Days of Summer* – and the writers were equally excited about him. "We didn't know anything about Marc at first, but we had the most remarkable marriage of ideas with him," says Neustadter. "All three of us very much wanted to make the same movie and that was exciting."

Adds producer Novick: "Marc is that rare director who doesn't sacrifice substance for style. He's stylish but all of his choices are specific, deliberate and used to forge a point of view."

Webb was, he says, highly energized by the challenge. "I came from a world were there are very few rules, where you're not as obligated to a strict narrative sensibility, and so you can break away from standard conventions. So I loved the idea of diving into a comedy that allowed itself to be non-linear and a little fantastical. The challenge for me was, within that, to find a way to keep the characters real enough that they engage people on a deep emotional level. You could say I wanted to find a line in this movie right between reality and magic."

THE MANY MOODS OF SUMMER: CASTING THE FILM

"Settle. Don't get too excited. She's just a girl. Wants to keep it casual.
Which is why she's in your bed right now. Without clothes. That's casual, right?"
— Tom

In *500 Days of Summer*, the typical "he said, she said" POV of romantic comedies is abandoned entirely in favor of the "he said" approach. Everything that is seen on screen comes straight from the love-addled, mood-clouded mind of Tom Hansen, a man who writes pithy romantic sayings for others yet can't seem to communicate the overpowering depth of his own feelings to the only women who matters to him: the elusive Summer.

Since all the other characters are ultimately viewed through Tom's subjective experience, casting Tom was central to the film's entire foundation. Director Marc Webb enthusiastically chose Joseph Gordon-Levitt, the young but already remarkably diverse actor who has distinguished himself over the last few years as uncategorizable and fascinating to watch in such films as *Stop-Loss, Miracle at St. Anna, The Lookout* and *Manic*.

"Joe is so very intelligent and he understood every line of this story and of Tom's entire emotional arc," says Webb. "At the same time, he was very inquisitive, asking a lot of great questions. It's easy to forget that Joe started his career on a sit-com, but he also has a very solid basis in the craft of comedy that he brings to Tom," says Webb. "He has an almost scientific approach to playing the straight man — he finds ways to be very funny while still bringing genuine emotion to every scene."

Gordon-Levitt loved the idea of telling a love story from the rarely cracked *male* interior point of view. "I liked that the story was written by two guys and is directed by a guy and they were all completely unapologetic about the idea that this story is from our perspective," he says. "It doesn't pretend to be an objective point of view. The entire story is completely subjective from Tom's internal experience and it illuminates his experience of love. Love isn't rational or logical or linear – and the film completely reflects that."

He continues: "It's a heartfelt cinematic experience that's hilarious but doesn't pander. It manages to be an authentic story about love without taking itself too seriously."

As for what Tom discovers about love in the midst of Summer, Gordon-Levitt says: "I think Tom always thought love was like what he saw in the movies or heard in pop songs. He has a lot of preconceived notions of what love should be, instead of really living in the present tense and paying attention to what's actually happening between him and Summer . . . which he only sees later."

Naturally, Gordon-Levitt was able to bring some of his own experience to the role. "I've had my heart broken before, truly, truly, truly broken," he confesses. "But when I look back at me in my broken-hearted phase it's pretty hilarious, because it feels so much more extreme than it really is. One of the things I love about *500 Days of Summer* is that it doesn't make light of what we go through in romances but it is honest about it and shows it for what it is, which is often profoundly funny."

Another joy for Gordon-Levitt was reuniting with Zooey Deschanel, with whom he previously starred as two disturbed teenagers in the indie drama *Manic*. "It was great to do something so completely different with her and to have fun every day," he says. "*500 Days* is so whimsical and dreamlike and sweet – and it's easy to feel like that when you're with Zooey."

Indeed, those qualities were precisely what led Marc Webb to cast the beguiling young actress, most recently seen in *Yes Man* with Jim Carrey, as Summer. "Zooey is just the perfect alt-ingénue," Webb muses. "She is Summer in so many ways. She's funny, she's real, she's very smart, she's got the most beautiful eyes you've ever seen and she's got a great sort of mercurial energy that makes her constantly compelling to watch."

Deschanel was drawn to the challenge of playing the ideal inside a young romantic's mind. "Summer is such an interesting character, because she's really seen entirely from Tom's perspective as this ideal woman, when she's actually just a smart, interesting girl with her own problems," she observes. "I was so excited when I read the script because it's so rare to see a romantic comedy that's really fresh and different. It felt like a new way of telling a story we think we've seen before."

Working with Gordon-Levitt was also a draw. "Joe and I have known each other for many years and I feel completely comfortable with him," she says. "I think he's the perfect Tom because he's sweet and adorable but he manages to communicate a kind of naiveté within all his charm."

What happens between Tom and Summer doesn't occur in a vacuum and it is Tom's friends and family who are his sounding boards and advisers through out the relationship as he tries to make sense of his desire for Summer and her not-always-clear responses. His two best friends – his doctor friend Paul and co-worker McKenzie – struggle to uncloud Tom's vision right from the get go. They are played by Matthew Gray Gubler, a young filmmaker and actor seen on CBS' "Criminal Minds," and Geoffrey Arend who has had memorable roles in such comedy hits as *Super Troopers* and *Garden State*.

"I see Paul and McKenzie as the kind of Good Angel and Bad Angel who are helping Tom to figure out what he's doing," says Gray Gubler. "Paul is more straight-laced and McKenzie is more rambunctious and so they're giving Tom completely divergent advice. Paul has been married for years to a girl he met in preschool and McKenzie has maybe dated one girl in his entire life. So, unfortunately, his two Obi Wan Kenobi's are on the socially inept side!"

Arend had a blast with the dynamic between Tom and McKenzie. "Tom is the eternal optimist, always waiting for Cinderella to sweep him off his feet and McKenzie is the pessimist who believes nothing is ever going to work, who believes true love is a myth," Arend notes. "But no matter what McKenzie or Paul says, Tom still always goes his own way."

Both actors were very intrigued by Marc Webb's innovative approach to story-telling. "It's a visual, mood-driven kind of storytelling that seems to get at what it feels like to be in love," sums up Gray Gubler. "And I love that it doesn't end on a cynical note."

Adds Arend: "I haven't encountered any story like this in recent memory that so closely gets at the clash between romance and reality. It busts through clichés and that's always interesting."

Providing perhaps Tom's best source of advice is, unexpectedly, his 12 year-old sister Rachel who dispenses such pull-no-punches gems as "just cause some cute girl likes the same bizzaro crap you do doesn't make her your soul-mate." To play Rachel, Webb cast young Chloë Grace Moretz, who has been acting since age 5 and has had roles in such features as *The Eye* and *Bolt*.

Tackling the brother/sister dynamic, Moretz says that she drew from plenty of real world experience. "I have four brothers of my own and they're all older, and I'm the only girl, so I know that chemistry," she says.

And, in spite of her age and relative inexperience in such matters, she was very clear on the uselessness of the state in which Tom finds himself. "When you're with somebody who is wearing rose-colored glasses you can see things they can't," Moretz explains. "That's how Rachel is with Tom. She sees things he doesn't and she's pretty fearless about speaking her mind."

THE SOUNDS OF SUMMER: ABOUT THE MUSIC

"I'm not near drunk enough to sing in front of all these people."
— Tom

Nothing can capture the slap-happiness of infatuation or the agony of heartbreak in a matter of minutes like a pop song – and music was always key to the vision for *500 Days of Summer*. Even as they wrote the screenplay, Scott Neustadter and Michael Weber were weaving specific tunes from their own memories – from Lee Greenwood's anthem "God Bless the USA" to a karaoke take on the Clash's plaintive "Train in Vain" to the ubiquitous Hall & Oates' ballad "You Make My Dreams Come True" — into the framework. Music is everywhere in the story; it's what draws Tom and Summer together; it's what fuels his ecstasy and charts his angst as he rides the roller coaster of their relationship; it's even what they bicker about, engaging in whimsical debate over their favorite Beatles.

"When you're falling in love or falling out of love, that's what you do. You listen to a massive amount of music," says Neustadter. "There's always a soundtrack to any relationship and songs are a great way to express certain feelings that can't be easily articulated."

Once Marc Webb came on board, he too envisioned the narrative unfolding not just visually but aurally, through a wall of sound that would further reflect the mad intensity and wonder of Tom's feelings – not to mention fantasies — about Summer. "Music is half of this movie and it's a way to affect people on a pure gut level," says Webb. "Coming from music videos, I've always been interested in how you apply images to music."

Music supervisor Andrea Von Foerster, who has worked on such hit music-driven shows as "The O.C." and "Grey's Anatomy," faced the challenge of securing the rights for songs that were important pieces to the final product – and finding additional songs, from classic and new artists, that would match Tom's kaleidoscope of feelings.

Von Foerster notes that the film was a dream project for a music lover. "Everyone involved in this film has fantastic musical taste, starting with the writers who wrote in so many great songs right into the story," she says. "That love of music has added another dimension to the storytelling."

THE LOOK OF SUMMER: DESIGNING TOM'S WORLDS, REAL AND FANTASIZED

"Relationships are messy and feelings get hurt. Who needs all that? We're young. We're in one of the most beautiful cities on earth. I say let's have as much fun as we can . . ."

— Summer

The imagery of *500 Days of Summer* streams directly out of Tom's inner experience of falling in love and fighting to stay in love when the going gets tough – and it runs the cinematic gamut from dream sequences to musical numbers to cartoon birds to odes to the melancholy of French films. As Marc Webb relates: "The idea was to create a complete world for Tom with its own space and time. We used a lot of different filmmaking tools and techniques, but we tried to avoid superficial gimmicks. The most important thing was always the emotional flow of the story."

Webb collaborated closely with cinematographer Eric Steelberg, who also shot *Juno*, frame by frame. "Marc's aesthetic was to be very natural but to punctuate that naturalism with these fantastical moments that show his heightened feelings surrounding Summer," Steelberg explains. "He also wanted to shoot Los Angeles in an original way and he showed me these really beautiful, tactile, moody color photographs of cities from the 50s and 60s and that was the style that he wanted to shoot in. For me, it was refreshing to work with a director who has such a strong sense of visual grammar and puts it as far forward as Marc does."

"We were interested in using color in a way that feels meaningful," says Webb. "Although we used a limited palette, we wanted it to still feel warm and inviting and artful."

Webb's idea to shoot Los Angeles as an iconic city of love like New York or Paris also greatly appealed to production designer Laura Fox. "We had an opportunity to create an unexpected view of Los Angeles," says Fox. "It's a city that can be very beautiful, romantic and exciting when you really look at the architectural details, and the buildings, and the history."

Adds Webb: "We were pretty vigilant in avoiding the clean, sleek and modern and using locations like pre-war downtown and Korea Town and the karaoke bar where you get this feeling of a world that's like a storybook left on the shelf – a little dog-eared, a little faded, but with lots of hope underneath."

Fox found the whimsy of the story an inspiration throughout her set designs. "This production was a lot of fun for me because there's this heightened reality to everything, so we were able to add twists to the real world, from Tom's stylish downtown loft to the greeting card company which is housed in an old dance hall. We gave everything a contemporary feel but also kept a timeless feel by using things that could have been used 20 years ago and will still be used 20 years from now."

Also going to town creatively was Hope Hanafin, the film's costume designer, who used a similar mixture of the timeless, the stylish and the romantic to further evoke Tom's world. Hanafin recalls Webb showing her photographs during their first meeting together that set the tone. "They were of contemporary subjects but had a feeling of being out of time. They had a monochromal quality and they were diffused enough that they had a sense of distance and romance," she recalls. "That was our starting point – looking for images that live in the imagination because they're not locked into any specific moment."

To get to that feeling, Hanafin created the character's costumes all in synch with each other, mixing and matching like a collage artist. She began with Tom, whose clothes shift with his emotions. She explains, "Tom is seen in more unkempt khakis and sweaters when he is at work where he's not as emotionally invested but when he is out and about and has the chance to be himself, he has a hipper, younger look that references the Sixties and French cinema."

She continues: "A lot of things play into his look and we were always looking at the interaction of his palette with all the other players so that things are either emphasizing or contradicting Tom's mood. Tom is always the pivotal person in every composition."

Indeed, Summer's look emerges from Tom's view of her as the ultimate object of his affection – hence her retro dresses, camisoles and hairstyles, that emphasize a distant memory of perfect femininity. But there was also something else that defined Summer... *the color blue*. Hanafin elaborates: "We saved the color blue just for Zooey's character. Zooey has the most amazing blue eyes and there's something magical about putting blue on her, or even putting blue behind her. No one else wears it except for one special moment . . . when the whole world turns blue."

Those kinds of color-bursting moments were vital to Marc Webb's vision for the film, but he also wanted them to be part and parcel of the storytelling. He summarizes: "I didn't want this movie to be about spectacle, but to break away from conventions and be an emotionally engaging journey about people figuring out the place of passion in their lives. I wish I'd known about Tom and Summer when I was 18 – maybe it would have made my love life a little easier!"

CAST AND CREW CREDITS

FOX SEARCHLIGHT PICTURES
Presents
a WATERMARK PRODUCTION Production

"(500) DAYS OF SUMMER"

JOSEPH GORDON-LEVITT   ZOOEY DESCHANEL
GEOFFREY AREND   CHLOË GRACE MORETZ   MATTHEW GRAY GUBLER
CLARK GREGG   RACHEL BOSTON   MINKA KELLY

Directed by
MARC WEBB

Production Designer
LAURA FOX

Casting by
EYDE BELASCO, CSA

Written by
SCOTT NEUSTADTER &
MICHAEL H. WEBER

Film Editor
ALAN EDWARD BELL

Unit Production Manager
JENNY HINKEY

First Assistant Director
RICHARD GRAVES

Produced by
JESSICA TUCHINSKY
MARK WATERS
MASON NOVICK
STEVEN J. WOLFE

Music Supervisor
ANDREA VON FOERSTER

Music by
MYCHAEL DANNA &
ROB SIMONSEN

Second Assistant Director
ERIC SHERMAN

Co-Producer
SCOTT G. HYMAN

Director of Photography
ERIC STEELBERG

Costume Designer
HOPE HANAFIN

Associate Producer
VERONICA BROOKS

CAST

Tom . . . . . JOSEPH GORDON-LEVITT
Summer . . . . . . ZOOEY DESCHANEL
McKenzie . . . . . . GEOFFREY AREND
Rachel . . . . CHLOË GRACE MORETZ
Paul . . . . MATTHEW GRAY GUBLER
Vance . . . . CLARK GREGG
Millie . . . . . . PATRICIA BELCHER
Alison . . . . RACHEL BOSTON
Girl at Interview . . . . . . MINKA KELLY
Millie's New Husband
. . . . CHARLES WALKER
Douche . . . . IAN REED KESLER
Bus Driver . . . . DARRYL ALAN REED
Employee #1 . . VALENTE RODRIGUEZ
New Secretary
. . . . YVETTE NICOLE BROWN
Partygoer . . . . NICOLE VICIUS
Another Partygoer . . . NATALIE BOREN
Rhoda . . . . MAILE FLANAGAN
Usher . . . . DARRYL SIVAD
Minister . . . GREGORY A. THOMPSON
Man . . . . MICHAEL BODIE
Mime . . . . JOHN MACKEY
Cupid . . . . JACOB STROOP
Wedding Singer . . . . . KEVIN MICHAEL
Grossman . . . . SID WILNER
Narrator . . . RICHARD MCGONAGLE
French Narrator . . JEAN-PAUL VIGNON
Stunt Coordinators . . . . AL GOTO
  JOHN KOYAMA
Stunts By: . . . . MARC SHAFFER
Choreographer . . . MICHAEL ROONEY
Assistant Choreographers
. . . . CHRISTIAN VINCENT
  TRACY PHILLIPS
Dancers . . . . BRYAN ANTHONY
  SYBIL AZUR
  CHERYL BAXTER
  GUS CARR
  JOHN CORELLA
  NADINE ELLIS
  ALEJANDRO ESTORNEL
  NATHANIEL FLATT
  RESHMA GAJJAR
  TIFFANY GRANATH
  JENNIFER HAMILTON
  BRANDON HENSCHEL
  MICHAEL W. HIGGINS
  KENNETH HUGHES

LEXY HULME
JOHN JACQUET JR.
JENNIFER KEYES
TIM LACATENA
REBECCA LIN
GELSEY WEISS MAHANES
KATIE MALIA
ANTHONY MARCIONA
CHRISTOPHER WAR MARTINEZ
VIVIAN NIXON
TRACY PHILLIPS
NATHAN PREVOST
JAMIE SHEA
RYAN THOMAS
CHRISTIAN VINCENT
JULL WEBER

MADE IN ASSOCIATION WITH DUNE ENTERTAINMENT III LLC

CREW

Art Director . . . . CHARLES VARGA JR.
Set Decorator . . JENNIFER LUKEHART
Leadman . . KEITH MCCARTHY-SMITH
On-Set Dresser. . . . . FELICE A. PAPPAS
Swing . . . . ANDREW BLUNDA
FRANK LEE DRENNEN
JASON D. DRURY
GARY SULLIVAN
Second Second Assistant Directors
. . . . AUDREY CLARK
MIKE CURRIE
PETE WATERMAN
Time Lapse Director of Photography
. . . . ZACHARY M. BOGGS
"A" Camera Operator/Steadicam Operator
. . . . MATTHEW MORIARTY
"A" Camera First Assistant
. . . . ZORAN VESELIC
"A" Camera Second Assistant
. . . . CRAIG M. BAUER
"B" Camera First Assistants
. . . . JASON GOEBEL
STEVEN CUEVA
"B" Camera Second Assistants
. . . . MILAN "MIKI" JANICIN
ANDERS A. YARBROUGH
"C" Camera Operator
. . . . JESSE M. FELDMAN
"C" Camera First Assistant
. . . . WALLY SWEETERMAN
"C" Camera Second Assistant
. . . . MICHELLE PIZANIS
Camera Loader . . . . SIMON ENGLAND

Still Photographers. . . CHUCK ZLOTNICK
ANTHONY FRIEDKIN
Sound Mixer . . . . . LORI DOVI, C.A.S.
Boom Persons . . . DAVID ALLEN SMITH
JEFF BLEHR
Cable Persons. . . . GEORGE B. GOEN II
BENJAMIN HOEKSTRA
Playback Operator . . JON M. TENDRICH
Property Master. . . . CYNTHIA NIBLER
Assistant Property Masters
. . . . MICHAEL VOELKER
MARK FINER
Script Supervisor
. . . . RENETTA G. AMADOR
Assistant Editor
. . . . JENNIFER VECCHIARELLO
Sound Design - Supervising Sound Editor
. . . . PIERO MURA
Sound Mixing
. . . . MATTHEW IADAROLA
GARY GEGAN
Gaffer . . . . ERIC FORAND
Best Boy Electric RICHARD BOTCHLET
Electricians . . . . . . ERIK GONZALES
TRAVIS STEWART
R. DUSTIN SANCHEZ
JOSHUA A. HICKS
DANNY VINCENT
OWEN FOYE
ALEXANDER TAYLOR
Rigging Gaffer. . . NEWTON TERMEER
Rigging Best Boy Electric
. . . . STEVE CHARNOW
Rigging Electricians . . . CHUCK SMITH
PATRICK A. TOOLE
Key Grip . . . . . DAVID RICHARDSON
Best Boy Grips . . . . DAN WELLS
ADAM CAMACHO
Dolly Grip. . . . . JOHN MANG
Company Grips . . . MYNOR PRIESING
JAMIE FRANTA
VADIM FRUMIN
VINCENT HALE
MATTHEW PERRY
AARON PRITCHARD
DARRYL ST. JUSTE
Rigging Key Grip
. . . . CHARLEY H. GILLERAN
Rigging Best Boy Grips
. . . . ROBERT ANDERSON
KEVIN FAHEY
Rigging Grips . . . . CARLOS DE PALMA
ANTHONY NEVAREZ
Costume Supervisor MARCY LAVENDER

Costumers . . . . SUMMER BROWNING	Assistant to Mr. Wolfe
RYCK SCHMIDT	. . . . MATTHEW RUBENSTEIN
Set Costumers . . . . . . CARRIE DACRE	Production Accountant
MICHELE JAFFE	. . . . GINTS KRASTINS
Cutter/Fitter . . . . . DANIELA KURRLE	Payroll Accountant
Make-Up Department Heads	. . . . TIMOTHY JOHNSTON
. . . . JORJEE DOUGLASS	Accounting Clerks . . KETT KETTERING
VANESSA PRICE	CRYSTAL CONNELL
Key Make-Up Artist	Assistant Production Coordinator
. . . . JAMIE LEIGH DEVILLA	. . . . BARBARA CASNER
Make-Up Artists . . . . SILVINA KNIGHT	Key Set Production Assistant
Hair Department Head	. . . . MICHAEL JUDD
. . . . DANIEL CURET	Set Production Assistants
Key Hairstylist/Personal Stylist to Ms.	. . . . JASON BRADFORD
Deschanel . . . . AARON LIGHT	JENNIFER ELLIS
Location Manager. . MICHAEL CHICKEY	TARA FISCHER
Key Assistant Location Managers	JESSAMYN LAND
. . . . MARTIN J. CUMMINS	JACOB LAWTON
JUSTIN DUNCAN	JASON ROBERTS
Assistant Location Manager. . TREY NEELY	Office Production Assistants
Production Coordinator . . MARK ASARO	. . . . LANCE KIRSHNER
Art Department Coordinator	CARL B. THOMPSON
. . . . PAULA THOMPSON	SEVE CANALES
Special Effects Coordinator	JOHN PALIFERRO
. . . . BOB GARRIGUS	Interns . . . . CRYSTAL JANET CHAVEZ
Digital Effects. . . HANDMADE DIGITAL	SARALEAH COGAN
Lead Compositor	DANIELLE COHEN
. . . . LEE "ROD" RODERICK	KANENE S. GRATTS
Compositors . . . . . . TODD GROVES	LIZA MARROQUIN
STEVE NEVIUS	CASSIOPEIA SMITH
Illustrator . . . . DION MACELLARI	Extras Casting . . MICHAEL SCHIAVONE
2D Bird Animation . . . DAVE SPAFFORD	ERIKA LEE
Bird Animation Compositing	Casting Associate
. . . . MONKEYWEED	. . . . JONATHAN RACKMAN
Construction Foreman. . . . STEVEN FOX	Unit Publicist. . . . . POLARIS PR
Scenic Artist. . . . . DIANA J. ZENG	Transportation Coordinator
Set Painter. . . . . R. ALARCON	. . . . MICHAEL PERROTTI
Carpenters . . . . CODY BARAJAS	Transportation Captain
LUIS F. CANDANOZA	. . . . JUAN J. RAMIREZ
JESUS FLORES JR.	Transportation Co-Captain
MADISON S. GIESSMANN	. . . . ERNESTO LUNA
MAXIMINO GONZALEZ	Caterer . . . . ANDRE DEVANTIER
MICHAEL LOPEZ	Chef . . . . FRANK PELLUCHON
SIMON MAYER	Craft Services . . HERNAN HERNANDEZ
TOMMY NOOCH	Concept Artist . . . . . . AMY UMEZU
CHAD SEIDE	Medic . . . . GREGG SPIEGELMAN
WYATT VANDERGEEST	Studio Teacher. . . . . . NANCY KLEIN
Assistant to Mr. Webb	Video Assist
. . . . NICHOLAS DUNLEVY	. . . . HARRY SANDLIN MATTICE III
Assistant to Ms. Tuchinsky	Libra Head Technicians . . DAVID HAMMER
. . . . KATE SULLIVAN	BRIAN MCPHERSON
Assistant to Mr. Waters. . CHRIS GOODWIN	Layout Board. . VERLA LOOMIS RANDALL
Assistant to Mr. Novick	Dialogue-ADR Supervisor
. . . . MICHELLE KNUDSEN	. . . . CHRIS WELCH, MPSE

Sound Effects Editor . . MARK MANGINI
Dialogue Editors
. . . . BETH STERNER, MPSE
JULIE FEINER
Foley Editor . . . . VALERIE DAVIDSON
Sound Editorial
. . TECHNICOLOR SOUND SERVICES
1ST Assistant Sound Editor
. . . . RONNIE MORGAN
Assistant Sound Editor . . . . ANDY SISUL
Sound Engineers . . . RODRIGO ORTIZ
STACEY DODDS
Foley Studios . . . . JRS PRODUCTIONS
Foley Artists . . . . JOHN SIEVERT
STEFAN FRATICELLI
Foley Mixers . . . . STEVE COPLEY
RON MELLEGHER
KEVIN SHULTZ
Foley Technical Assistance
. . . . RYAN LUKASIC
ADR Stages
. . TECHNICOLOR SOUND SERVICES
LARSON STUDIOS
ADR Facility Coordinator
. . . . ANDREA M. METTY
ADR Mixers . . . . JUDAH GETZ
STACEY MICHALES
ANDREW MORGADO
Voice Casting . . . . BARBARA HARRIS
Titles & Day Slate Sequences by
. . . . IMAGINARY FORCES
End Titles By . . . . . . FIX IT IN POST
Digital Intermediate Facility . . COMPANY 3
Digital Intermediate Colorist
. . . . DAVE HUSSEY
Digital Intermediate Project Manager
. . . . NICK MONTON
Digital Intermediate On-Line Editor
. . . . JIM EBERLE
Color Timer . . . . DALE GRAHN
Music Coordinator . . . . . LAURA WEBB
Supervising Music Editor . . JEN MONNAR
Temp Music Editor . . . DORIAN CHEAH
Additional Music By . . . . . . AMRITHA
FERNANDES+BAKSHI
Score Recorded & Mixed by
. . . . BRAD HAEHNEL
Assistant Engineer . . . . PATRICK SPAIN
Dolby Sound Consultant
. . . . BRYAN ARENAS
Camera Dollies by . . CHAPMAN/LEONARD
STUDIO EQUIPMENT, INC.
Script Clearance Research provided by
. . . INDIECLEAR, CAROL COMPTON

Financing Provided By
. . . . CITY NATIONAL BANK
RICHARD V. MCCUNE AND
ERIK PIECUCH

US
Written and Performed by Regina Spektor
Courtesy of Sire Records
By arrangement with Warner Music Group
Film & TV Licensing

THE BOY WITH THE ARAB STRAP . .
Written by Sarah Martin, Stuart Murdoch,
Richard Colburn, Michael Cooke,
Christopher Geddes,
Stephen Jackson and Isobel Campbell

THERE IS A LIGHT THAT NEVER
GOES OUT
Written by Johnny Marr and Steven
Morrissey
Performed by The Smiths
Courtesy of Warner Music U.K. Ltd.
By arrangement with Warner Music Group
Film & TV Licensing

BAD KIDS
Written by Cole Alexander, Ian Brown, Jared
Swilley and Joseph Bradley
Performed by Black Lips
Courtesy of Vice Records
By arrangement with Zync Music Inc.

SHE'S LIKE THE WIND
Written by Patrick Swayze and Stacy Wideliltz
Performed by Patrick Swayze Featuring
Wendy Fraser
Courtesy of The RCA Records Label
By arrangement with SONY BMG MUSIC
ENTERTAINMENT

PLEASE, PLEASE, PLEASE, LET ME GET
WHAT I WANT
Written by Steven Morrissey and Johnny Marr
Performed by The Smiths
Courtesy of Warner Music U.K. Ltd.
By arrangement with Warner Music Group
Film & TV Licensing

EVERY ROSE HAS ITS THORN
Written by Bobby Dall, C.C. Deville, Bret
Michaels and Rikki Rockett
Courtesy of Turn Up The Music, Inc.
Under license from Downtown Music LLC

SUGAR TOWN
Written by Lee Hazlewood
Courtesy of Stingray Music

SHE'S LIKE THE WIND
Written by Patrick Swayze and Stacy Widelitz
Courtesy of Turn Up the Music, Inc.
Under license from Downtown Music LLC

HERE COMES YOUR MAN
Written by Charles Thompson
Courtesy of Stingray Music

GOD BLESS THE U.S.A.
Written by Lee Greenwood
Courtesy of Turn Up The Music, Inc.
Under license from Downtown Music LLC

HAVE I BEEN A FOOL?
Written and Performed by Jack Peñate
Courtesy of XL Recordings Ltd.

THERE GOES THE FEAR
Written by James Goodwin, Andrew Williams and Jeremy Williams
Performed by Doves
Courtesy of EMI Records Ltd./Capitol Records
Under license from EMI Film & Television Music

YOU MAKE MY DREAMS
Written by Sara Allen, Daryl Hall and John Oates
Performed by Daryl Hall and John Oates
Courtesy of The RCA Records Label
By arrangement with SONY BMG MUSIC ENTERTAINMENT

KNIGHT RIDER (MAIN TITLE)
Written by Glen Larson and Stuart Phillips

SWEET DISPOSITION
Written by L. Sillitto and A. Mandagi
Performed by The Temper Trap
Courtesy of Liberation Music

QUELQU'UN M'A DIT
Written and Performed by Carla Bruni
Courtesy of Sheridan Square Entertainment

VENI VIDI VICI
Written by Cole Alexander, Ian Brown, Jared Swilley and Joseph Bradley
Performed by Black Lips
Courtesy of Vice Records
By arrangement with Zync Music Inc.

THE MUSIC
Written by Chad Howat, JT Daly and Andrew Smith
Performed by Paper Route
Courtesy of Universal Records
Under license from Universal Music Enterprises

TRAIN IN VAIN (Stand By Me)
Written by Topper Headon, Mick Jones, Paul Simonon and Joe Strummer
Courtesy of Stingray Music

MUSHABOOM
Written by Leslie Feist
Performed by Feist
Courtesy of Universal International Music, B.V.
Under license from Universal Music Enterprises

AT LAST
Music by Harry Warren
Lyrics by Mack Gordon
Performed by Kevin Michael
Kevin Michael performs courtesy of Downtown Records/Atlantic Recording Corp.

HERO
Written and Performed by Regina Spektor
Courtesy of Sire Records
By arrangement with Warner Music Group Film & TV Licensing

THE INFINITE PET
Written by Britt Daniel
Performed by Spoon
Courtesy of Merge Records
By arrangement with Bank Robber Music

BOOKENDS
Written by Paul Simon
Performed by Simon & Garfunkel
Courtesy of Columbia Records
By arrangement with SONY BMG MUSIC ENTERTAINMENT

VAGABOND
Written by Myles Heskett, Chris Ross and Andrew Stockdale
Performed by Wolfmother
Courtesy of Interscope Records
Under license from Universal Music Enterprises

SHE'S GOT YOU HIGH
Written by James "Tate" Arguile, Niall Buckler, Oli Frost, Gareth Jennings and James "Noo" New
Performed by Mumm-Ra
Courtesy of SONY BMG MUSIC ENTERTAINMENT (UK) LIMITED
By arrangement with SONY BMG MUSIC ENTERTAINMENT

THE PRODUCERS WISH TO THANK THE FOLLOWING FOR THEIR ASSISTANCE:
Permission for display of Neutra sketches courtesy Dion Neutra, Architect © and Richard and Dion Neutra Papers, Department of Special Collections, Charles E. Young Research Library, UCLA
The UCLA Bruin Marching Band
Film footage from THE GRADUATE used with permission of StudioCanal
Footage From 'STAR WARS' (1997) Courtesy of Twentieth Century Fox.
All rights reserved.

KODAK FILM STOCK... PANAVISION LOGO Deluxe Logo
DOLBY STEREO (logo)
DTS SDDS

Approved No 45018

Copyright © 2009 Twentieth Century Fox Film Corporation and Dune Entertainment III LLC in all territories except Brazil, Italy, Japan, Korea and Spain.
Copyright © 2009 TCF Hungary Film Rights Exploitation Limited Liability Company, Twentieth Century Fox Film Corporation and Dune Entertainment III LLC in Brazil, Italy, Japan, Korea and Spain.

500DS Films, Inc. is the author of this motion picture for purposes of copyright and other laws.
The events, characters and firms depicted in this photoplay are fictitious. Any similarity to actual persons, living or dead, or to actual events or firms is purely coincidental.
Ownership of this motion picture is protected by copyright and other applicable laws, and any unauthorized duplication, distribution or exhibition of this motion picture could result in criminal prosecution as well as civil liability.

©2009 TWENTIETH CENTURY FOX. ALL RIGHTS RESERVED. PROPERTY OF FOX. PERMISSION IS GRANTED TO NEWSPAPERS AND PERIODICALS TO REPRODUCE THIS TEXT IN ARTICLES PUBLICIZING THE DISTRIBUTION OF THE MOTION PICTURE. ALL OTHER USE IS STRICTLY PROHIBITED, INCLUDING SALE, DUPLICATION, OR OTHER TRANSFER OF THIS MATERIAL. THIS PRESS KIT, IN WHOLE OR IN PART, MUST NOT BE LEASED, SOLD, OR GIVEN AWAY.

About the Filmmakers

MARC WEBB (Director) directs stuff. Short films, videos, commercials, drinking games. Whatever. He has won several MTV VMAs™ including 2006 Best Rock Video for AFI's "Miss Murder" and Best Group Video for The All-American Rejects' "Move Along." The Music Video Production Association honored him in 2006 as the Director of the Year for his work with Weezer, AAR, and My Chemical Romance. *500 Days of Summer* is Webb's first feature.

He likes penne pasta and hates to be called "chief" or "buddy."

His short film *Seascape* premiered at the Aspen Comedy Festival, which is funny, because he didn't think it was funny. So, to ensure he wouldn't make another comedy, he went to Baghdad to direct a documentary on the first day of school in post-war Iraq. But people laughed at him there too.

Webb studied at Colorado College, NYU for a semester, and Art Center for a few months. He received a Newberry Fellowship and spoke at his graduation. The person next to him told him to shut up.

His dad is a mathematician and his mother is a biologist. His brother just had another baby. Her name is Isabelle. Marc has pictures if you want to see.

SCOTT NEUSTADTER & MICHAEL H. WEBER (Writers) met in 1999 when Weber applied for an internship and Neustadter hired him for the job. Since selling their first pitch in 2005, they have written projects for Sony, Universal, 20th Century Fox, Paramount, and Fox Searchlight, including two feature films — the semi-autobiographical *500 Days of Summer* and the not-at-all autobiographical *Pink Panther 2*.

Neustadter hails from Margate, New Jersey, and currently lives in Los Angeles. He loves sad British pop music and the movie *The Graduate*. Weber was born in Manhattan and refuses to leave. Ever. They were recently named "10 Writers to Watch" in *Variety*.